DELICIOUS, HEALTHY, SUGAR-FREE

DELICIOUS, HEALTHY, SUGAR-FREE

How to create simple, superfood recipes
to increase energy and lose weight

PATRICK HOLFORD *and*
FIONA McDONALD JOYCE

piatkus

PIATKUS

First published in Great Britain in 2008 by Piatkus Books as *Food GLorious Food*

Published in Great Britain in 2017 by Piatkus as *Delicious, Healthy, Sugar-Free*
1 3 5 7 9 10 8 6 4 2

A CIP catalogue record for this book
is available from the British Library

ISBN 978-0-349-41445-4

Printed and bound in China by C&C Offset Printing Co, Ltd
Design: Emil Dacanay and Sian Rance for D.R. ink
Recipe photography © Ian Greig Garlick
Home economist: Lorna Brash

Papers used by Piatkus are from well managed forests and other responsible sources

MIX
Paper from
responsible sources
FSC® C104740

Piatkus
An imprint of
Little, Brown Book Group
Carmelite House
50 Victoria Embankment
London EC4Y 0DZ

An Hachette UK Company
www.hachette.co.uk

www.improvementzone.co.uk

Picture credits
Ian Greig Garlick: pp. 8, 11, 12, 20, 27, 35, 43, 46, 49, 50, 52, 54, 56, 58, 60, 62, 64, 66, 68, 74, 79, 84, 91, 99, 104, 109, 113, 114, 119, 122, 125, 129, 133, 136, 138, 142, 147, 151, 155, 159, 165, 170, 177, 181, 186; Corbis: pp. 28, 31, 36, 40, 44, 53, 57, 61, 65.

Acknowledgements

Patrick

I would like to thank my wife, Gabrielle, who has travelled the world with me, trying out new foods, and supporting me in my busy work and teaching schedule; Ruth, for her help with the research; and the wonderful team at Piatkus/Little, Brown, particularly Gill, Jillian and Jo, for their commitment to getting this important information out to you, the reader, and for making such a beautiful book.

Fiona

I would like to thank all of my friends who have stoically waded their way through endless meals, giving much appreciated feedback on recipes. Particular thanks are due to my husband Nick, for his endless enthusiasm, and to my editors, Gill, Jillian and Jo, at Little, Brown.

Foreword

Let me first congratulate you on choosing this book. Not only will it help you achieve optimal health and prevent chronic disease, but it will show you how to do this while still enjoying delicious meals and snacks every day of the week. Everyone knows that an apple is a better snack than potato crisps. But do you know that a daily handful of walnuts and a bowl of berries can help improve your health and wellbeing and increase your lifespan? Or that becoming a 'pescatarian' – that is, basing your protein intake mostly on fish and shellfish – can help your mind, heart, joints, skin and digestion?

Backed by proven research on the importance of eating a low-glycemic diet, which in essence means combining the right type and amount of carbohydrate-rich foods with the right type and amount of proteins and fats, *Delicious, Healthy, Sugar-Free* provides you with the knowledge and tools to enjoy more energy, longevity and protection against chronic disease.

With the advent of fast-food chains and TV dinners, the importance of fresh, unadulterated food has been forgotten by too many. But, little by little, there is a resurgence of interest in – and a commitment to – choosing our food wisely and healthily, as farmers' markets and wholefood stores grow in popularity and more and more organic foods are sold in supermarkets.

Delicious, Healthy, Sugar-Free will help you make a major step forward in embracing the food–health connection, which is so perfectly summarised in the maxim 'let food be your medicine and medicine be your food'. First postulated by Hippocrates, the father of Medicine, almost 2500 years ago it was right then, and it is right – and even more necessary – today. Food is not just a form of sustenance, it can actually promote good health. Instead of worrying about the foods you should avoid, *Delicious, Healthy, Sugar-Free* invites you to actually embrace healthy foods and 'superfoods' from around the world and welcome them as your best allies on your way to a long and healthy life.

In my practice as a specialist in Internal Medicine I focus on the prevention and treatment of lifestyle-related metabolic diseases like obesity, diabetes, heart disease and inflammatory conditions, and have witnessed the fantastic benefits of a low-glycemic, balanced diet first-hand, having included it in the treatment of over 12,000 of my patients. I know that it has worked for them, and those who have read my books, and I know that it will work for you too.

Using 'nature's own pharmacy' – easily accessible in the fresh produce section of your supermarket – and the knowledge and inspiration of *Delicious, Healthy, Sugar-Free*, you'll find it easy to cook delicious, wholesome meals that will delight even the pickiest palate.

Delicious, Healthy, Sugar-Free is a treat for the senses and it will revolutionise the way you think about healthy eating. Enjoy!

Dr Fedon Alexander Lindberg

Specialist in Internal Medicine and Metabolic Disorders and author of 'The Greek Doctor's Diet' book series

Contents

Introduction

You Can Have Your Cake and Eat It

What if you could discover a range of truly delicious foods and recipes that not only left you satisfied, full of energy and feeling really good, but also prevented 21st century diet-related diseases such as obesity, diabetes and heart disease? The aim of this book is to make that 'what if' a reality. It's designed for people who enjoy their food, and love cooking and entertaining, but who also take a keen interest in their own health and the health of their family and friends.

There's absolutely no reason why healthy food has to be tasteless and dull. After all, the basis of good nutrition is simple, fresh, high-quality ingredients, which provide maximum flavour as well as maximum nutrients. That's why we have been particularly excited and inspired by the wonderful cuisines of other cultures, especially those that make excellent use of fresh herbs and spices. These add fantastic flavours, so you don't need to add as much salt, and also impart nutritional benefits, such as aiding digestion or helping to fight infections.

We've found, for example, that two favourites of Southern Indian cooking – tamarind and turmeric – keep you slim, and protect the brain and joints from inflammation. Likewise, we've discovered that shiitake mushrooms, which are used widely in Japan, where cancer rates are a fraction of those of the west, give your immune system a boost. Fiona shares our findings in the Foods for Family and Friends section (see pages 48–69), which takes you on a trip around the world and examines 'superfoods' and cooking methods from different countries.

Of course, not all foods are easy to find everywhere, but there are plenty of recipes here that use local ingredients, plus suggestions for ingredients that can be substituted where these are unavailable. Choosing local foods, preferably in season, helps to reduce your carbon footprint, but we also encourage you to opt for organic and free-range produce, because they are a more direct route to the end goal of delicious food that's good for you.

The majority of the recipes have a low glycemic load (GL) – the significance of which is explained in Part One – to help anyone who is watching their weight or trying to boost their energy levels. Eating a low-GL diet is not only the best way to stay lean, but it's also proven to prevent diabetes, heart disease and cancer (see www.holforddiet.com/evidence for the scientific details). However, this is not a diet book and there are no rules or menu plans to follow slavishly. We believe eating should be an actively pleasurable experience and we believe it should positively promote health, too, so this is a book to dip into when you want to cook food for friends and family that will make you all feel GLoriously good!

Bon appetit!
Patrick Holford and Fiona McDonald Joyce

PART ONE
THE HEALTH BIT

by Patrick Holford

What Is a Well Balanced Diet?

Back in 1984, when I founded the educational charity the Institute for Optimum Nutrition (ION), my colleagues and I, free from the bias of vested interests, started researching the question 'what is a well-balanced diet?'

In the largest ever survey of this type carried out in Britain, we studied the diets and health of 37,000 people to work out which foods give you health and which take it away. The chart below shows you which foods have a consistently positive effect (fruit, vegetables, oily fish, seeds, nuts and water) and which foods have a consistently negative effect (sugary foods, caffeinated drinks, red meat, wheat, dairy products, refined foods and salt) on different aspects of health.

Defining the Optimum Diet

	Overall health	Energy	Stress	Hormones	Mind & mood	Digestion	Detox	Immunity	Skin
Sugary foods	✕✕	✕✕	✕✕	✕✕	✕✕	✕✕	✕✕	✕✕	✕✕
Tea/coffee/cola	✕✕	✕✕	✕✕	✕✕	✕✕	✕✕	✕✕	✕✕	✕
Red meat	✕✕	✕✕	✕	✕✕	✕✕	✕✕	✕✕	✕✕	✕✕
Wheat (bread, pasta etc.)	✕✕	✕✕	✕	✕✕	✕✕	✕✕	✕✕	✕✕	✕✕
Dairy (milk, cheese etc.)	✕✕	✕✕	✕	✕	✕✕	✕	✕✕	✕	✕
Refined foods	✕✕	✕✕	✕	✕✕	✕	✕✕	✕✕	✕✕	✕✕
Salt	✕✕	✕✕	✕	✕	✕	✕✕	✕✕	✕✕	✕
Fruit	✓	✓✓	✓	✓✓	✓✓	✓✓	✓✓	✓✓	✓✓
Vegetables/salad	✓	✓		✓	✓✓	✓	✓	✓	✓
Oily fish	✓✓	✓✓		✓	✓	✓		✓	✓
Seed/nuts	✓✓	✓✓		✓		✓✓		✓✓	✓
Water	✓✓	✓✓	✓	✓✓	✓✓	✓	✓✓	✓	✓

✕✕ Strongly negative   ✕ Negative   ✓✓ Stongly positive   ✓ Positive

Source: ONUK Survey, ION (see www.ion.ac.uk/onuksurvey to download the survey for free)

The Optimum Diet Pyramid

Fat
A handful of ground seeds and nuts and a dessertspoon of cold-pressed oil per day

Protein
3 servings per day of beans, lentils, quinoa, tofu (soya) or 'seed' vegetables. Alternatively replace one of these with a small helping of fish, a free-range egg or lean meat. Have dairy products (cheese, milk) infrequently

Complex carbohydrates
4 servings per day of whole grains, such as brown rice, millet, rye, oats, corn, quinoa, and infrequently wholemeal bread or pasta

Fruit and vegetables
6 or more servings per day of fruit and vegetables. Eat citrus fruit, apples, pears, berries and melons. The best vegetables are dark green, leafy and root vegetables

This is just some of the research that has fed into our definition of what eating a well-balanced diet really means. Our conclusions, 30 years on, are shown in the Optimum Diet Pyramid above, which is quite different from the watered down government guidelines that we think are part of the health problem, not the solution.

While for many people the kind of diet represented by this pyramid is not going to be achievable overnight, it does give a clear indication of where you should be heading. To help you understand how the main constituents of our diet – and the choices we make within those categories – affect our health let's look at each of these in turn.

About fat

There are two main kinds of fat: saturated and unsaturated. Saturated fat, which is usually hard fat, is not essential and we should eat it seldom, if at all. The main sources are meat and dairy products, although a different and healthier kind of saturated fat is found in coconut. However, saturated fat has one advantage: it doesn't generate harmful oxidants when it's heated, for example when it's used for frying, which is why, as you'll see, we sauté foods in coconut oil or butter, as well as olive oil.

There are also two kinds of unsaturated fats: monounsaturated fats, found in olive oil, and polyunsaturated fats, found in nut and seed oils, and fish. As well as containing some essential fats, olive oil is very versatile, with proven health benefits, yet it is more stable than polyunsaturated or 'very' unsaturated fats. Some polyunsaturated fats are essential, though, including linoleic acid (an omega 6 fat) and alpha linolenic acid (an omega 9 fat). These are vital for the brain, nervous system, immune system, cardiovascular system and skin.

The optimal diet provides a balance of essential omega 3 and omega 6 oils. Pumpkin and flax seeds are rich in omega 3, while sesame and sunflower seeds are rich in omega 6. These essential fats are easily destroyed by heating or exposure to oxygen, so eating raw, fresh sources on a daily basis is important. However, by far the most potent omega 3 fats are those found in oily fish, so in Part Two you'll find lots of delicious recipes that include fish.

Processed foods often contain hardened or 'hydrogenated' polyunsaturated fats. These are unhealthy and best avoided completely. So, too, are deep-fried foods, where the frying process has turned the fats into damaged 'trans' fats.

To achieve your optimal intake of the right kind of fats:
- Eat 1 tablespoon of cold-pressed seed oil (sesame, sunflower, pumpkin, flax seed etc.) or 1 heaped tablespoon ground seeds each day
- Eat oily fish three times a week
- Sauté foods in coconut oil, olive oil or butter
- Avoid deep-fried food, burnt or browned fat and any food containing hydrogenated fat
- Reduce your intake of meat and dairy products

About protein

Protein is made out of amino acids, which are the building blocks of the body in much the same way as words are made out of letters. As well as being vital for growth and the repair of body tissue, amino acids are used to make hormones, enzymes, antibodies and neurotransmitters, and they help transport substances around the body. Both the quality of the protein you eat, which is determined by the balance of these amino acids, and the quantity are important.

The best quality protein foods in terms of amino acid balance include eggs, quinoa (a grain that cooks like rice), soya, beans, lentils, fish and meat. Vegetable protein sources tend to contain more beneficial complex carbohydrates than meat, plus animal protein sources tend to contain a lot of undesirable saturated fat as well, so it's best to limit your meat intake to three times a week and pick your meat carefully, choosing lean, fit, preferably organic meat. Many vegetables, especially 'seed' foods such as runner beans, peas and broccoli, contain good levels of protein. They also help to neutralise excess acidity, which can lead to the loss of minerals, including calcium. Frequent meat eaters have a higher risk of osteoporosis because a high meat intake causes acidity and in order to counteract this the body leaches calcium from the bones.

To achieve your optimal intake of protein:
- Eat three servings of either quinoa, tofu (soya), beans, lentils, 'seed' vegetables or other vegetable protein, such as nuts or seeds, a day
- Occasionally replace one of these servings with fish, cheese, a free-range egg or lean meat
- Limit meat and cheese to three times a week
- Avoid excess animal protein

About carbohydrate

Carbohydrate is the body's main fuel. It comes in two forms: fast-releasing, as in sugar, honey, malt, sweets and most refined foods, and slow-releasing, as in whole grains, vegetables and fresh fruit. The latter foods contain more complex carbohydrates and more fibre, both of which help to slow down the release of sugar. This gives them a lower glycemic load, or GL (GL is explained in detail on pages 21–24).

Fast-releasing or high-GL carbohydrates are best avoided, as constant use of fast-releasing carbohydrates can give rise to complex symptoms and health problems. Some fruits, like bananas, dates and raisins, contain high-GL sugars and are best kept to a minimum, especially if you have weight issues or diabetes. You'll see we use alternative sweeteners such as xylitol, a natural sweetener found in some fruit and vegetables, and agave syrup, a low-GL, syrup-like sweetener. Low-GL carbohydrates – vegetables, fresh fruit, pulses and whole grains – should make up about half of your diet. Vegetables are better for you than fruit, because they are very low in sugar yet very high in nutrients. Especially good are dark green leafy vegetables, which are high in B vitamins. Two servings of vegetables with each main meal and two servings of fresh fruit gives you six servings a day.

Eating these kinds of foods in such quantities will also give you at least 35g of fibre, which is an ideal daily intake. Fibre absorbs water in the digestive tract, making the food contents bulkier and easier to pass through the body, preventing constipation and the putrefaction of foods. This also slows down the absorption of sugar into the blood, helping to maintain good energy levels.

To achieve your optimal intake of carbohydrate:
- Eat three or more servings of dark green, leafy and root vegetables, such as spinach, carrots, sweet potatoes, broccoli or peppers, raw or lightly cooked, a day
- Eat three or more servings of fresh fruit, such as apples, pears, plums, cherries, berries, melon or citrus fruit, a day
- Eat bananas infrequently
- Eat four servings of whole grains, such as brown rice, millet, rye, oats, whole wheat, corn, quinoa or pulses, a day
- Avoid any form of sugar, foods with added sugar, and white or refined foods

What this all boils down to is five simple guidelines for healthy eating, summarised in the following box.

Top Five Diet Tips

Every day make sure you eat:

- I heaped tablespoon of ground seeds or I tablespoon of cold-pressed seed oil
- 3 servings of vegetable protein
- 3 pieces of fruit
- 3 servings of leafy or root vegetables
- 4 servings of whole grains

The when and how of eating

It isn't just what you eat that counts, but how and when you eat it. Here are five tips that will help you get more goodness out of your food:

- **Graze, don't gorge**
  Studies have consistently shown that people who eat little and often are healthier than those who just eat one or two large meals a day. In practice, for most people this means having breakfast, lunch and dinner plus a couple of snacks in between. That way you'll provide your body with a constant and even supply of fuel, which means you'll experience fewer food cravings.
- **Breakfast like a king, lunch like a prince, dine like a pauper (or a prince)**
  There's a lot of truth in this old saying, although it needs a little modification. Firstly, you need food for energy during the day, so it doesn't make sense to eat half your daily intake of food in the evening. Also, it's definitely not a good idea to go to bed while you're still digesting your dinner. As a general rule, you should eat dinner early and wait at least two hours before going to sleep.
- **Chew your food thoroughly**
  Chewing your food and eating at regular times really helps you to digest and get the most out of your food. After all, your stomach doesn't have teeth.
- **Eat something raw with every meal**
  The healthiest diet has a large proportion of raw or very lightly cooked food.

- **Eat fruit as a snack and have a dessert as a treat**

  Unlike protein-rich foods, fruit doesn't need to be digested in the stomach and will pass rapidly through the stomach for digestion further on in the digestive tract. If you eat a fruit salad after a piece of chicken the fruit will have to stay in the stomach longer than it needs to and may ferment. For this reason, it's generally better not to have fruit or a fruit-based dessert immediately after a protein-rich main course, or at least make sure you have a reasonable break between courses.

Why Low-GL Eating Means High-level Health

Balanced blood sugar is an important component in maintaining health and central to this is the food you eat on a daily basis.

When your blood sugar is low, you will feel tired and hungry, although the symptoms of low blood sugar can also include poor concentration, irritability, nervousness, depression, sweating, headaches and digestive problems. If you refuel with fast-releasing, high-GL carbohydrates, you cause your blood sugar to rise rapidly. Your body doesn't need that amount of sugar all at once, so it dumps the excess into storage as fat. Then your blood sugar goes down again. This vicious cycle of yo-yoing blood sugar then leads to permanent tiredness, weight gain and carbohydrate cravings.

An estimated three in every ten people have an impaired ability to keep their blood sugar level stable. The result, over the years, is that they are likely to become increasingly fat and lethargic. However, if you can control your blood sugar levels, the result is even weight and constant energy.

The secret of stable blood sugar

Fast-releasing carbohydrates are like rocket fuel, releasing their glucose in a sudden rush. They give a quick burst of energy followed by a rapid burn-out. So if you want to balance your blood sugar, you need to eat fewer fast-releasing foods – sweets and anything made with white flour, including cakes and biscuits – and more slow-releasing foods – wholegrain carbohydrates, fresh fruit and vegetables.

Fast or slow: the GL guide

The best way to achieve a stable blood sugar balance is to control the glycemic load (GL) of your diet. You may have heard of the glycemic index (GI) or know about the connection between restricting carbohydrates and weight loss. Well, GL develops these concepts to the next stage, to create a scientifically superior way of controlling blood sugar.

The reason I focus on the carbohydrate content of foods is because the other two main food types – fat and protein – don't have a significant effect on blood sugar. In fact, I recommend that you eat some fat and protein with your carbohydrate, because this will further lessen the effect the carbohydrate has on your blood sugar, thereby lowering the GL of your meal. To this end, you'll find that the menus in this book are balanced to give a protein food, such as fish, with a carbohydrate-rich food, such as rice.

Understanding GL

GL combines the GI with the concept of measuring carbohydrate intake to provide a scientifically superior way of controlling blood sugar. Put simply, the GI of a food tells you whether the carbohydrate in the food is fast- or slow-releasing. It's a 'quality' measure. It doesn't tell you, however, how much of that food is carbohydrate. Carbohydrate points, or grams of carbohydrate, on the other hand, tell you how much of a food is carbohydrate, but don't tell you what that particular carbohydrate does to your blood sugar. They are a 'quantity' measure. The GL of a food is the quantity times the quality, so it combines these two measures to give an accurate indicator of the impact a serving of a particular carbohydrate has on your blood sugar.

Opposite are some examples of high- and low-GL carbohydrates, so you can understand which kind of foods to choose, and why the recipes in Part Two feature certain types of carbohydrate foods (see www.holforddiet.com for a complete list of foods and their GL scores). Ideally you want to eat 5GLs for a snack and 7 to 10GLs for the carbohydrate portion of a main meal. If you want to lose weight you should aim for 40GLs a day or 60 to maintain your weight. In the chart, the moderate-GL foods are marked with a single asterisk and the high-GL foods with two. Note: if you are wondering why some of the foods that have a GL of 5 are marked as high GL, remember that serving size is important so a bagel is a high GL food but you can restrict yourself to 5GLs and still have some – but only if you eat a quarter of one.

Food	Serving looks like	GL
Fruit		
Blueberries	large punnet (600g)	5
Apple	1 small (100g)	5
Grapefruit	1 small	5
Apricot	4 apricots	5
Grapes	10 grapes	5
Pineapple	1 thin slice	5
Banana*	1 small	10
Raisins**	20	10
Dates**	2	10
Starchy vegetables		
Pumpkin/squash	large serving	7
Carrot	1 large	7
Beetroot	2 small	5
Boiled potato*	3 small (60g)	5
Sweet potato*	1 (120g)	10
Baked potato*	1 (120g)	10
French fries**	10	10
Grains, breads and cereals		
Quinoa	65g (2/3 cup cooked)	5
Pearl barley	75g (cooked)	5
Brown basmati rice*	small serving (70g)	5
White rice**	1/2 serving (66g)	10
Couscous**	1/2 serving (66g)	10
Rough oatcakes	2–3	5
Rye pumpernickel-style bread	1 thin slice	5
Wholemeal bread*	1 thin slice	5
Bagel**	1/4 bagel	5
Puffed rice cakes**	1 rice cake	5
White pasta	small serving (78g)	10
Beans and lentils		
Soya beans	31/2 cans	5
Pinto beans	1 can	5
Lentils	large serving	7
Kidney beans	large serving (150g)	7
Chickpeas	large serving (150g)	7
Baked beans*	large serving (150g)	7

* Moderate GL ** High GL

Breaking the sugar habit

The taste for concentrated sweetness is often acquired in childhood. If sweet things are used as a reward or to cheer someone up, they become emotional comforters. The best way to break the habit is to avoid concentrated sweetness in the form of sugar, sweets, sweet desserts, dried fruit and neat fruit juice. Sweeten breakfast cereals with fresh fruit, and have fruit instead of sweet snacks. If you gradually reduce the sweetness in your food, you will get used to the taste of foods without added sugars.

However, beware of switching to natural sugars such as honey or maple syrup as these still cause a rapid increase in blood sugar. Artificial sweeteners are not so great, either, as some have been shown to have harmful effects on health and all perpetuate a sweet tooth. As I've said, one of the best sugar alternatives is xylitol, the vegetable sugar that has a very low GL. It tastes much the same as regular sugar, but doesn't raise blood sugar significantly. Nine teaspoons of xylitol, for example, have the same effect as just one teaspoon of regular sugar or honey. Another low-GL sweetener is agave syrup. You will find both these sweeteners used in some of the recipes in Part Two.

To balance your blood sugar, which will help you achieve stable energy levels and regulate your weight:
• Choose low-GL foods
• Eat protein alongside carbs
• Graze rather than gorge
• Avoid refined carbohydrates and sugary foods

The Perfect Balance for Energy and Weight Control

The rewards of eating a diet that optimises rather than depletes your health are many – more energy, great skin, sharper mind, better mood, trouble-free digestion, less illness and better weight control. I've already talked about the best types of carbohydrate, protein and fat to eat and the fundamental low-GL diet principles for eating, but what does all this look like on your plate?

The illustration below provides a basic template to follow when you're preparing lunch or supper. Protein should make up one quarter of your meal; starchy carbohydrates, such as rice, potatoes, pasta or bread (in other words those that contain more sugar), another quarter; and half of your plate should be fresh, low-carbohydrate vegetables or salad.

How to Balance What's on Your Plate

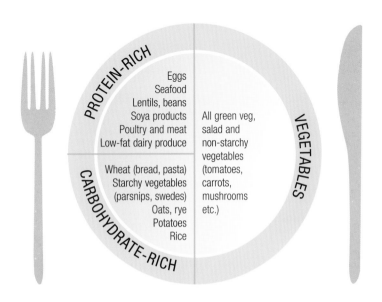

PROTEIN-RICH

Eggs
Seafood
Lentils, beans
Soya products
Poultry and meat
Low-fat dairy produce

VEGETABLES

All green veg, salad and non-starchy vegetables (tomatoes, carrots, mushrooms etc.)

CARBOHYDRATE-RICH

Wheat (bread, pasta)
Starchy vegetables (parsnips, swedes)
Oats, rye
Potatoes
Rice

Choosing carbohydrates

As you are probably beginning to realise, not all carbs are created equal. For optimal health, eat slow-releasing carbohydrates – in other words those with the lowest GL score. To help you decide what to put on the 'starchy carbohydrate' quarter of your plate here are some examples of those with a GL of 7, as that's what I recommend for people trying to lose weight. If you just want to maintain your weight, you can increase the portion sizes suggested by about a third to 10GLs.

Starchy carb	7GLs looks like	10GLs looks like
Pumpkin/squash	large serving (186g)	double regular serving (266g)
Carrot	1 large (158g)	2 regular (266g)
Swede	regular serving (150g)	large serving (214g)
Quinoa	regular serving (120g)	large serving (188g)
Baked beans	large serving (150g)	double serving (214g)
Lentils	large serving (175g)	double serving (300g)
Kidney beans	large serving (150g)	double serving (214g)
Pearl barley	small serving (95g)	regular serving (136g)
Wholemeal pasta	half serving (85g)	large serving (112g)
White pasta	third serving (66g)	small serving (78g)
Brown rice	small serving (70g)	regular serving (84g)
White rice	third serving (46g)	half serving (66g)
Couscous	third serving (46g)	half serving (66g)
Sweetcorn	half a cob (60g)	1 small cob (88g)
Boiled potato	2 small (74g)	3 small (106g)
Baked potato	1 medium (59g)	1 large (84g)
French fries	6–7 (47g)	8–10 (68g)
Sweet potato	half (61g)	1 small (88g)

You can enjoy non-starchy vegetables in unlimited quantities as their starch, or sugar, content is minimal. Aim to fill half your plate with:

alfalfa	raw carrot	kale	rocket
asparagus	cauliflower	lettuce	runner beans
aubergine	celery	mangetout	spinach
beansprouts	courgette	mushrooms	spring onions
beetroot	cucumber	onions	tenderstem
broccoli	endive	peas	tomatoes
brussel sprouts	fennel	peppers	watercress
cabbage	garlic	radish	

Eat More Superfoods

Not all foods are created equal. Some foods are especially loaded with anti-ageing antioxidants and other key health promoting nutrients. These are called superfoods.

Superfoods are used as much as possible in the recipes in this book and you can read about them in detail in Part Two, but they include:

Beans	Pomegranate	Spinach
Blueberries	Pumpkin seeds	Tomatoes
Broccoli	Quinoa	Turmeric
Oats	Salmon	Walnuts
Oranges	Soya	Yoghurt

Berry good for you

In the short list of superfoods above you'll have seen blueberries, which have the highest antioxidant content of all fruits due to their anthocyanidin bioflavonoids, but, in fact, most berries have health-giving properties. For instance, all berries are excellent at boosting the immune system in the fight against colds and flu and you may be surprised to learn that strawberries have more vitamin C than oranges. Strawberries and raspberries also contain ellagic acid, which helps protect against cancer, and the quercetin in strawberries helps strengthen blood vessels and reduce bruising, too. Cranberries are also very high in quercetin, a natural anti-inflammatory. This is

all to say that, when possible, you should eat a serving of berries every day, although cherries are as good as berries, because they're high in antioxidants, but low in GL. Pomegranate also contains anti-inflammatory polyphenols, including ellagic acid, to protect against cancer and heart disease.

What's the Best Food for Vitamin C?

Vitamin C-rich foods	Amount per 100g
Broccoli	110mg
Peppers	100mg
Kiwi fruit	85mg
Lemons	80mg
Brussels sprouts	62mg
Papayas	62mg
Cabbage	60mg
Cauliflower	60mg
Strawberries	60mg
Tomatoes	60mg
Watercress	60mg
Oranges	50mg

You'll notice that peppers come high up in the list above and all peppers are an excellent source of vitamin C. However, hot peppers, from which we get chilli, cayenne and paprika, are rich sources of capsaicin. This is a natural anti-inflammatory and may protect you from intestinal infections. Provided you are not allergic to them, which some people are, spicy foods are good for you.

Eat your greens and beans

One of the most important B vitamins is folate. As it's name suggests, it's high in 'foliage', as in green leafy vegetables. However, you may be surprised to learn that lentils, beans, nuts and seeds are just as good, if not better, sources of folate. Ideally, you need to take in 400mcg of folate each day, so these foods need to become a regular part of your diet. You're simply not eating enough folate-rich foods if you didn't eat something like one of the following four menus yesterday:

• A salad with Romaine lettuce, endive, half an avocado and a handful of sunflower seeds, accompanied by a glass of orange juice
• Spinach and lentil or millet bake with a serving each of broccoli and parsnips
• A fruit salad with papaya, kiwi fruit, orange and cantaloupe melon in orange juice, plus a handful of unsalted peanuts
• An orange, a large serving of broccoli, spinach or Brussels sprouts, and a bowl of miso soup

What's the Best Food for Folate?

Folate-rich foods	Amount per 100g
Wheatgerm	325mcg
Lentils, cooked	179mcg
Millet flakes	170mcg
Sunflower seeds	164mcg
Endive	142mcg
Chickpeas, dried, cooked	141mcg
Spinach	140mcg
Romaine lettuce	135mcg
Broccoli	130mcg
Kidney beans	115mcg
Brussels sprouts	110mcg
Peanuts	110mcg
Orange juice, fresh or frozen	109mcg
Asparagus	98mccg
Hazelnuts	72mcg
Avocados	66mcg

Eating greens, and especially broccoli, tenderstem (a cross between Chinese kale and broccoli) and cruciferous vegetables, such as cabbage, cauliflower, kale and Brussels sprouts, is especially important because they are also rich sources of potent anti-cancer and detoxifying nutrients. Broccoli is particularly rich in DIM (Di-indol-methane), which mops up excess oestrogen, thereby reducing the risk of breast and prostate cancer.

Eat a multi-coloured rainbow diet

The table overleaf shows you which foods are especially high in anti-ageing antioxidants. The simplest way to ensure a good intake is to eat a multi-coloured diet. This is because different colours contain different kinds of antioxidants, hence a rainbow diet gives you the best all-round protection. Each day eat something:

Orange, such as carrots, squash, sweet potatoes or oranges. Carrots also contain pectin to help remove toxins and oranges are an excellent source of both vitamin C and folic acid.

Red, such as tomatoes or red onions. Tomatoes contain cancer-preventing lycopene and are another excellent source of vitamin C. Red onions are especially high in quercetin, the powerful anti-inflammatory that, among other properties, can help to reduce allergic sensitivity.

Yellow, such as yellow squash, turmeric or mustard. Turmeric contains the natural painkiller curcumin, which may also help prevent cancer.

Green, such as asparagus, avocado, artichoke, greens, broccoli or peas. These have many proven health benefits.

What's the Best Food for Antioxidants?

Antioxidant-rich food	Per 100g	Per serving
Cinnamon	267536	7134 (1 tsp)
Turmeric	159277	7964 (1 tsp)
Mustard powder	29257	1462 (1 tsp)
Dark chocolate	13120	3936 (30g)
Beans, kidney	8459	8459 (1/2 can)
Blueberries	6552	6552
Plums	6259	3755 (2)
Blackberries	5347	5347
Garlic	5346	535
Raspberries	4882	9764
Bilberry	4460	4460
Strawberries	3577	7154
Cherry	3365	1683
Broccoli	3083	1542
Apple	3082	3082 (1 small)
Pomegranate	3037	1516
Potatoes, sweet	2115	2538 (1 small)
Avocado	1933	1450 (1/2)
Orange	1819	2183 (1 large)
Kale	1770	177
Beetroot	1767	1767
Grapefruit, pink	1548	3096 (1 small)
Spinach, raw	1515	1515
Grapes, red	1260	1260 (15)
Tenderstem	1183	592
Onion	1034	1034 (1 medium)
Brussels sprouts	980	490
Alfalfa sprouts	931	931
Beans, baked	904	904
Kiwi fruit	882	882
Pepper, red	791	791
Sweetcorn	728	874 (1 cob)
Carrots, raw	666	1066 (1 large)
Peas, frozen	600	300
Yellow squash	396	990
Cantaloupe	315	473 (1/2 small)

Source: US Department of Agriculture, Agricultural Research Service, Beltsville Human Nutrition Research Center, 2007

Superfood secrets

Although it's probably not as visually appealing as most of the antioxidant-rich foods, the unassuming grain-like seed quinoa is a superfood with a powerful punch. It looks and boils like rice, but the protein in it is of the highest quality, equivalent to that in meat and just as good as soya, although soya has a higher percentage of protein per serving. Unlike meat, which is largely protein and fat, quinoa contains low-GL carbohydrate, fibre, protein and a little polyunsaturated fats, so all in all it's a much better, balanced food.

Likewise, the plain appearance of oats tends to mask their almost magical properties, but oats are one of the lowest GL carbohydrates, and they keep blood sugar balanced and help prevent diabetes. Oats, or specifically oat bran, contain a powerful anti-diabetes nutrient called beta-glucans. Diabetic patients given oatmeal or oat bran-rich foods experience much less pronounced rises in blood sugar. In fact, if 10 per cent of your diet consists of beta-glucans, it can halve the blood sugar peak of a meal. Practically, that means eating an equal mix of oat flakes and oat bran, cold or hot as porridge, and snacking on rough oat cakes, which contain the most beta-glucans. With over 1000 studies on beta-glucans, the evidence really is overwhelming.

On the surface, seeds can also be seen as fairly unprepossessing, but they undoubtedly qualify as a superfood. Chia and pumpkin are probably the best, being rich in omega 3, plus zinc and magnesium. Chia is also a great source of soluble fibres. But all beans, nuts and seeds are high in protein plus plant sterols, which help lower cholesterol. By combining with carbohydrates they even out your blood sugar, appetite and weight. The type of omega 3 in seeds is not, however, nearly as potent as that found in oily fish, particularly fish with teeth, that is fish that eat fish, and fish that live in cold water. These are exceptionally high in omega 3 fats, particularly those called EPA, DPA, and DHA, which are proven to reduce your risk of heart disease and boost your brain power. They are also an excellent source of both protein and mind-boosting phospholipids, which are needed to build nerves and brain cells, including the brain's memory molecule, acetylcholine. My advice is to eat oily fish three times a week.

Cholesterol-busting foods

Going back to cholestrol, the combination of eating oats, high in beta-glucans, and beans, nuts and seeds, high in plant sterols, helps to lower your cholesterol naturally. In a study designed by Professor David Jenkins (the man who invented GI), 34 patients with high cholesterol were placed on a low-fat diet, a low-fat diet plus statins (cholesterol-lowering drugs), and a diet high in plant sterols and soluble fibres.[1] Each patient had to do each diet for a month, although the diets were assigned in random order. On the high plant sterols/soluble fibre diet, the patients ate the equivalent of 2.5g of plant sterols in the form of 50g of soya (a glass of soya milk, a small serving of tofu or a small soya burger); 35g of almonds (a small handful); or 25g of soluble fibres from oats and vegetables (the equivalent of five oatcakes, plus a bowl of oats and three servings of vegetables).

Both statins and the plant sterols/soluble fibre diets significantly lowered LDL cholesterol – the 'bad' type of cholesterol – to the same degree, but nine of the volunteers (26 per cent) achieved their lowest LDL cholesterol while on the plant sterols/soluble fibre diet, not the statins. However, while statins lower levels of LDL cholesterol, they are relatively ineffectual at raising levels of HDL – the 'good' type of cholesterol. So, to sum up, eating the kind of superfoods used in the recipes in this book is likely to lower your cholestrol more effectively than any drug.

Finally on the topic of cholestrol, one of the most prevalent myths in nutrition is that eating eggs raises your cholesterol and therefore increases your risk of heart disease. This is not true. Eggs are an excellent source of both protein and brain-boosting phospholipids. Having said that, eggs are at least half fat and whether that's good fat or bad fat depends entirely on what you feed the chicken. For this reason I strongly suggest you avoid any non-free range eggs and ideally choose eggs labelled as high in omega 3, because that means the chickens have either been fed flax seeds or fish meal. I recommend you eat six eggs a week.

Eat Less Wheat and Dairy

Bread may be a staple food for you, but for many it's more of a 'cereal killer' than a 'staff of life'. The reason is that wheat contains a protein called gluten and, specifically, a type of gluten called gliadin, which is exceedingly unfriendly to your digestive tract.

People who are extremely sensitive to wheat will eventually develop a digestive tract that's as flat as a pancake, because all the tiny protrusions, called villi, which create the massive surface area of your insides, are destroyed. This is called coeliac disease and it affects approximately one in a hundred people (although many medical textbooks wrongly say one in 4,000).[2] Far more people, and this may possibly include you, have a less severe allergy to, or intolerance of, wheat.

So how do you know if you are one of those people? There are two ways to find out. You can take a proper food allergy test, a blood test that checks for the presence of the immunoglobulin G (IgG), an antibody that tends to have a delayed reaction, appearing in the blood up to 48 hours after you have been exposed to the allergen. Alternatively, you can avoid wheat for ten days and see how you feel. If you follow the latter course of action and find that you feel much better at the end of ten days, but worse when you reintroduce wheat, I recommend you have an IgG blood test to see whether you do actually have an allergy to wheat and, if you do, whether you have an allergy to any other foods, too (see page 184 of Resources).

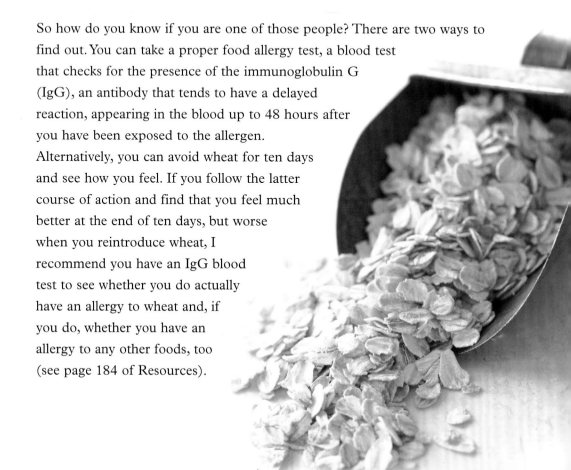

The Common Symptoms of Gluten Allergy

If you suffer from any of these conditions, you may have a gluten allergy:

- Sniffling, snuffling and sinus problems
- Fatigue and chronic fatigue syndrome
- Mouth ulcers
- Anaemia
- Diarrhoea or constipation
- Abdominal bloating
- Crohn's disease or diverticulitis
- Depression
- Poor concentration and brain 'fog'

The problem protein – gluten

Gluten is the key protein in wheat, but it's also found in rye, barley and oats. In fact, gluten is a name for a family of proteins found in grains. The principal type of gluten, called gliadin,[3] is found in wheat, along with glutenin, but rye and barley also contain chemically similar types of gluten, called hirudin and secalin respectively, so a person who is sensitive to wheat is also likely to react to barley and rye. Oats are quite different, however, because the type of gluten in oats bears no resemblance to the gliadin in wheat.

Approximately 80 per cent of people diagnosed with coeliac disease don't react to oats.[4] About one in three people who have an IgG test for food allergies will react to wheat. Of these, 90 per cent will react to gliadin, whereas 15 per cent will react to barley and 2 per cent will react to rye. Even fewer react to oats. Most people's immune systems react to gliadin when it gets into the bloodstream and that means you may be affected, which is why it's important to eat a diet that isn't built around wheat.

How it all began

Humankind started eating grains containing gluten, at the earliest, 10,000 years ago or, to put it another way, if the history of humankind was condensed into 24 hours we would have been eating grains for, at most, six minutes. In fact, some cultures only started to eat wheat in the last 100 years – or the last two seconds. As grains are a relatively new food for the human race, it could explain why as many as one in three people in Britain may be allergic to gluten.

Research shows that at least 15 per cent of wheat-eaters do have gliadin in their blood. Of course, if you don't eat wheat very often, and have impeccable digestion and a super-healthy digestive tract that stops any undesirables getting through, no gliadin is going to get into your bloodstream. However, people who don't digest so well can retain gliadorphins, which are wheat-based opioids, in their blood.[5] According to the research of Dr Paul Shattock at Sunderland University, these can actually make you crave the wheat products you are allergic to.[6]

All this means it is generally a good idea to eat fewer gliadin grains, such as barley, rye, spelt and especially wheat, and more non-gliadin grains, such as amaranth, buckwheat, corn, gram (ground chickpea flour), maize, millet, oats, quinoa and rice. Although some of the recipes in this book use gliadin grains for taste and variety, a number of non-gliadin grains are also featured and wheat is used sparingly.

Milk is a four-letter word

If you were still breastfeeding at the age of 30 wouldn't you consider that rather strange? That's actually what we all do by drinking milk – not only that but we're breastfeeding from another species! Put this way, it may not be so surprising that our immune system often reacts against milk and we have difficulty digesting it. The most common food allergy is to milk. Many people have an immediate reaction, as their body produces the antibody immunoglobulin E (IgE), but a delayed reaction, in which the body produces IgG, is also common.

Logically, milk's status as a gut irritant and an allergen isn't surprising, since it's a highly specific food, containing all kinds of hormones designed for the first few months of a calf's life, and, like wheat, it's also a relatively recent addition to the human diet. Our ancestors, after all, didn't milk buffaloes. Once we have been weaned, approximately 75 per cent of people (25 per cent of Caucasians and 80 per cent of Asian, Native American or African origin) stop producing lactase, the enzyme that's needed to digest the milk sugar, lactose.[7] Between 18 months and four years after birth, most Asian, Hispanic, Afro-American, Native American and Caucasians of southern European descent gradually lose lactase, which is one of many clues that the human body isn't designed to drink cow's milk, at least beyond early childhood.

Of course, most of us have been brainwashed into believing that milk is not only a necessary food, but also something approaching a wonder food, yet half the world, for example most of China and Africa, survives, and even thrives, without it. What's more, the more milk you drink, the greater your risk of a wide range of common diseases, including breast, prostate and colo-rectal cancer.[8] Milk is certainly a reasonably good source of calcium, among other nutrients, but drinking milk certainly isn't the only or necessarily best way to achieve optimal nutrition – you can get plenty of calcium from other foods, including seeds, nuts and beans.

The Common Symptoms of Milk Allergy or Lactose Intolerance

If you suffer from any of these conditions, you may have a milk allergy or lactose intolerance:

- Poor sleep
- Asthma
- Bronchitis
- Chronic fatigue
- Depression
- Diarrhoea
- Eczema

- Frequent infections
- Headaches or migraines
- Heartburn
- Hyperactivity
- Indigestion
- Rheumatoid arthritis
- Rhinitis and sinus problems

If you have some of these symptoms, notice what happens when you avoid all dairy products. If your symptoms clear up, I recommend you investigate the possibility that you have a milk allergy.

Milk is present in most butter, cream, cheese, yoghurt and ice cream, and is hidden in all kinds of food. Sometimes it's called milk protein, sometimes casein, which is the predominant type of protein – and the most allergenic – in dairy products, and sometimes whey, which is milk protein with the casein removed. You'll be amazed at how many foods contain milk, from bread and cereals to packaged food and crisps.

However, there are many dairy-free options and alternatives. For example, try rice, almond, quinoa or soya milk; coconut milk, butter or cream; pumpkin seed butter; non-hydrogenated vegetable oils and spreads, which haven't been treated to make them solid at room temperature (a process which increases their unhealthy saturated fat content); soya yoghurt; or cashew cream, which is made by blending cashew nuts with rice milk. Again, many of these foods feature in the recipes in this book.

Nutritious Food for Budding Vegetarians

You don't have to be vegetarian to be optimally nourished and you can achieve optimum nutrition as a vegetarian. However, whether you're a vegetarian or not, it's a good idea to increase your intake of vegetable-based foods and reduce or cut out red meat, which is often high in saturated fat.

Red meat, unless organic or wild game, is likely to come from animals that have been treated with antibiotics or hormones and these can end up in the meat you eat. Many people start by avoiding red meat, choosing fish or chicken in place of it, and, provided you choose fit, free-range chickens, there are only benefits to eating in this way.

Fishy business

The next step for some is to become a pescatarian (someone who eats fish but no other 'meat'). This is probably the easiest way to achieve an optimal intake of all nutrients, since fish is a good source of the omega 3 fats that can otherwise be quite hard to come by. Omega 3 fats are particularly high in salmon, tuna, herring and mackerel. Eating fish two or three times a week is one way to achieve an optimal amount of these nutrients, plus vitamins B_{12} and D, and protein, none of which are found in plant foods. For these reasons there are a number of fish recipes in the book.

However, fish is not without its potential problems. Fish caught in polluted waters transfer that pollution to the person who eats them, although frozen fish is usually caught in the farther reaches of oceans, so it's less likely to be polluted. Scavengers, including crab, lobster and shellfish, scour the sea bed for food and if they're caught in polluted waters, they can accumulate pollutants such as toxic heavy metals. On the other hand, shellfish from unpolluted waters are incredibly high in nutrients. Oysters, for example, contain 148mg of zinc per 100g, compared to Brazil nuts which, despite being one of the richest plant foods for minerals, provide 4.2mg per 100g.

Farmed fish are often treated with antibiotics and other undesirable chemicals, but there are tighter controls on the use of antibiotics in organic fish farming, as well as what the fish are fed and overcrowding. Carnivorous fish (those with teeth) are more likely to contain larger amounts of omega 3 fats, but squid, octopus, shrimps and prawns contain a larger proportion of saturated fat, so it's better to limit your intake of these. In short, though, when it comes to fish, don't skimp on quality.

Fish are best poached or baked, rather than fried, as these cooking methods are less likely to destroy their essential fats. Smoked fish is also OK. This process involves slowly cooking the fish by placing them on racks through which heat and wood smoke passes, but as the flesh inside isn't oxidised by the smoke, it isn't greatly damaged.

Vegetarian and vegan diets

The word 'vegetarian' applies to people who eat plant-based foods, plus eggs and dairy produce. While, generally speaking, it is considered healthy to be a vegetarian, many vegetarians actually eat quite an unhealthy diet by relying too much on wheat (bread, cereal and pasta) and dairy products (cheese, milk and yoghurt). As I've explained, these food groups are the two most common food allergens, but if you react badly to milk products, you may discover you can tolerate yoghurt more easily, as the bacteria in it digest the lactose and turn it into lactic acid, and you may also find that goat's or sheep's milk products have no or fewer adverse effects. Both eggs and dairy products are good sources of vitamin B_{12} and vitamin D, as well as protein. However, vegetarians need not rely on these as their only source of protein, as there is plenty of protein in beans, lentils, seeds, nuts and grains, especially rice, soya and quinoa.

Vegans, of course, go one step further and avoid all animal produce, including dairy products and eggs. Again, this can be completely compatible with optimum nutrition – it just means more care needs to be taken to consume all the right nutrients. The two nutrients lacking in a vegan diet are vitamin B_{12} and vitamin D. Some bacteria produce vitamin B_{12}, so fermented food, such as yoghurt made from soya milk, can provide a source. It's also claimed that vegans shouldn't scrub their organic vegetables, because

the bacteria in soil can also be a source of B_{12}. However, the trouble is that earth enriched with manure can also contain undesirable micro-organisms. While our ancestors may have obtained some B_{12} in this way, it's probably a lot easier, safer and better to take a multivitamin that provides both vitamin B_{12} and vitamin D.

Vegans and vegetarians also need to eat seeds, especially flax or chia seeds, to obtain sufficient omega 3 essential fats. Chia seeds are the richest source of omega 3 fats, followed by flax and pumpkin seeds. I recommend a tablespoon a day, preferably ground up and sprinkled on cereal, salad or soup, as the grinding helps make the nutrients more available. This is especially important for women who are pregnant or breast-feeding, as their babies need omega 3 fats to build a healthy brain and nervous system. In fact, I would recommend vegan mothers break their rule and take a fish oil supplement, which will give them the omega 3 fats EPA and DHA, or find a vegetarian supplement derived from seaweed that provides EPA and DHA.

Vegans also need to make sure they get around 40 grams of protein a day, so it is especially important to eat three to four servings of beans, lentils, quinoa, tofu or seeds on a daily basis. Grains such as rice also contain protein, but not as much as beans or lentils. In reality, the best way to achieve the right amount on a vegan diet is to have a good tablespoon of seeds on a grain-based breakfast cereal, plus two main meals, each with a substantial amount of either beans, lentils, quinoa or tofu. Some of the recipes in this book are vegan and hence suitable for vegetarians as well, plus, where possible, we have included dairy-free substitutes for dairy products.

The Best Cooking Methods

Cooking food for long periods or at high temperature depletes nutrients. It also increases the rate at which the carbohydrate content will be released, because cooking starts to break it down (this is why an eight-minute steamed new potato has a lower GL score than a 70-minute oven-baked potato). Raw food is almost always the most nutritious food, but when you need to cook, the healthiest methods are steaming, poaching, steam-frying, boiling, baking and grilling – in that order. Avoid frying food as much as possible and stay away from deep-frying as if you life depended on it – because it does!

Raw eating: Salad and fruit are not the only foods to enjoy raw. Raw vegetable sticks served with a dip are a great way to start a meal and vegetable juices provide a potent nutrient hit. You can even make raw soups, such as the delicious Spanish soup Gazpacho (see page 96).

Steaming: Instead of boiling your vegetables, steam them in a steamer, basket or even a colander over a pan of boiling water with a lid on top. This will preserve a lot more of their vitamins, as well as enhancing their flavour. You can also steam fish, especially oily varieties, as this method doesn't damage the essential fats they contain.

Steam-frying: It's simple to do – just put a little oil into a pan that has a lid and sauté your food for a minute, then add a water-based sauce (such as a little vegetable stock, soya sauce, white wine or just some water) and put on the lid. The liquid prevents the oil getting too hot and your food cooks fast, but retains all its taste. This is a great way to cook stir-fries and vegetables.

Baking and grilling: These methods are both useful ways of cooking fish or meat, but bear in mind that browning food creates harmful substances (oxidants), so avoid oil where possible and don't cook for too long.

Microwaving: Although it's quick, microwaving destroys more nutrients than steaming and can really damage essential fats, so avoid cooking oily fish this way. Microwaves also give off electromagnetic radiation, which some research has found to be harmful.

PART TWO
THE DELICIOUS BIT

by Fiona McDonald Joyce

Food for Family and Friends

If you think you have to take a night off from healthy eating when cooking for friends or that party food is incompatible with good nutrition, then think again. In this book, chocolate mousse, cheesecake, brownies, risotto, fish cakes, casseroles and many other wonderful dishes have been given an optimum nutrition makeover and are all firmly on the menu.

Standard dinner party fare has a reputation for being decadent; dripping in butter and cream, packed with refined grains or oozing with sugar. In the recipes that follow however, I show you how to prepare a delicious feast without resorting to creamy sauces and sugar-laden concoctions. To this end, I make use of the wealth of different ingredients and cooking techniques from around the world that are now at our disposal, from curries and stir-fries to Mediterranean mezze, as well as drawing on great British classics such as roasts with all the trimmings and tempting tea-time treats.

FOREIGN FLAVOURS

The standard Western diet suffers from repetition. We tend to over-eat the same foods, relying on refined wheat products such as bread, pasta, pizza, cakes and biscuits and dairy products such as milk, cheese and yoghurt. Lack of variety in your diet is a recipe not only for boredom, but also for digestive problems, particularly from these hard-to-process wheat and dairy products. They are abrasive on the gut lining, so regular consumption strains the digestive system. If your cooking is stuck in a repetitive rut, experiment with different cooking styles from around the world to expand both your repertoire of meals and your intake of nutrients. Herbs, for example, are underused by many Western cooks, yet these delicious and healthy ingredients are fully utilised in Eastern and much Mediterranean cooking for their flavour and health-giving properties.

This book allows you to explore foods from all over the world; everywhere from Thailand to the Mediterranean by way of the Middle East. The following section features individual cuisines, highlighting the 'superfoods' from each culture, as well as any dietary pitfalls that you should take care to avoid.

INDIAN

INDIAN FOOD OFTEN gets unfairly damned as being fattening and heavy. It's true that the white rice and naan bread accompaniments are high in starch, so I recommend that you avoid these and choose small portions of wholegrain versions instead, such as brown basmati or low-GL rice, and parathas or chapatti flatbreads, which are usually made from wholemeal flour. Rich, creamy sauces like korma and pasanda are high in fat, but other aspects of Indian cooking are, in fact, extremely nutritious.

The strong vegetarian influence means that many dishes feature pulses and fresh fruit and vegetables, all of which are high in fibre, vitamins and minerals and low in saturated fat. In tandoori dishes for example, meat is marinated in spices or yoghurt and skewered over a coal tandoor, sealing in flavour while draining off fat. Tomato-based sauces like rogan josh and madras are also low in fat, plus the tomato sauce is rich in lycopene, the antioxidant that helps protect skin from ultraviolet damage as well as helping to prevent macular degeneration.

The biggest contributor to the fat content of Indian dishes is, of course, the ghee or clarified butter used for frying. Its high saturated fat content serves a valuable purpose, however, as it is capable of being heated to very high temperatures without burning, making it a very safe fat to cook with. Use ghee in moderation for authenticity or follow my lead and replace it with coconut oil, which is even more stable when heated and which has a plant-based fat structure, which doesn't lead to weight gain.

The characteristic Indian spices not only add flavour and colour to dishes, but some also have remarkable health benefits. Here are the key players for optimum nutrition, Indian-style.

TAMARIND PASTE: This sticky pulp from inside the bean-pod of the tamarind tree has a sweet and sour flavour that works particularly well with fish. You'll find it in Oriental stores, possibly in the pod, or as jars of paste in the international section of good supermarkets. Tamarind is rich in potassium, which helps to control blood pressure and fluid retention.

TURMERIC: The 'golden spice of India' is used in everything from curry powder to medicines, as it is antiseptic and anti-inflammatory. Curcumin, the active ingredient in turmeric and what gives it its brilliant yellow-ochre colour, is a powerful antioxidant that can protect the body from damage by free radicals – presumably the reason why Indians dip fish in the spice before frying. Use it in curries or add to rice, couscous and quinoa dishes during cooking to give colour and flavour.

CINNAMON: The bark of the cinnamon tree is available in its dried tubular form, known as a quill, or as ground powder. The essential oils in this warming, sweet spice have been found to contain active components which have anti-blood clotting actions, reduce inflammation, inhibit the growth of bacteria and yeasts, and help blood sugar control. It features in many of our recipes, including Raw Chocolate and Goji Granola (see page 78).

COCONUT: The flesh and milk of the coconut are used in many Indian dishes. It is also a traditional remedy, due largely to its high lauric acid content, which is antibacterial and antiviral. Though coconut oil is very high in saturated fat, this is a plant-based saturated fat, which is used as energy rather than being stored as fat in the body, like animal fats. Being saturated, it is also very stable and isn't damaged by the cooking process to form harmful free radicals. Use desiccated coconut in biscuits and cakes such as the Pear and Coconut Cake (see page 168), coconut milk in curries and coconut oil for frying, as recommended throughout this book.

CHILLI: This hot spice is packed with vitamins A and C, both of which are powerful antioxidants and immune system boosters. In fact, chillies contain more vitamin C than citrus fruits. To get all the flavour but less heat, remove the white seeds and membranes. Chilli has been associated with reducing congestion and with pain relief, as well as with aiding digestion.

LENTILS: Dahl is a standard accompaniment to hotter Indian curries and it's often made from lentils, although split peas and mung beans are also used. The mild, savoury flavour of the pulses counterbalances the highly spiced curry. Lentils also contain fibre, protein and significant amounts of magnesium and folic acid.

THAI

THE FABULOUSLY FRAGRANT, flavoursome herbs and spices that make Thai cuisine so popular are not just delicious, they also have powerful health-giving properties. Many of the herbs featured in Thai cooking are particularly beneficial to digestion and Thai meals traditionally start with a digestion-boosting broth such as tom yum soup. Steaming and stir-frying are common cooking methods, ensuring minimal loss of nutrients during the cooking process. Thai cuisine is also ideally suited to anyone who needs to avoid dairy products, as it tends to use coconut milk rather than cream in sauces. Watch out for the sticky rice that accompanies curries and stir-fries though, as its high starch content will upset blood sugar levels. Simple boiled white rice or noodles are less starchy, but watch the portion size. Key Thai superfood ingredients include:

MANGO: Mangoes start off green and develop patches of red, yellow or gold as they ripen. When squeezed gently they should be soft, but not squidgy, to the touch. Thanks to their orange fresh, they are rich in the antioxidant vitamin betacarotene, as well as vitamin C, vitamin E and iron.

GALANGAL: Similar in appearance to ginger, galangal provides a distinctive flavour and aroma in Far Eastern cuisine. Frequently featuring in fish and shellfish recipes, often with garlic, ginger, chilli and lemon or tamarind, you can find it in Oriental grocery stores. It is thought to improve digestion and reduce wind, help nausea, reduce inflammation and aid circulation.

HOLY BASIL: Also known as tulsi, this traditional Thai herb is often used in stir-fries with chilli and garlic, and has revered medicinal properties. An antioxidant and anti-inflammatory, it is also an adaptogen, which means it helps the body cope with stress, plus it is thought to aid bloating. However, it's not widely available everywhere, so seek it out in specialist stores.

CORIANDER: Thai cooking makes use of all parts of the coriander plant, not just the leaves (used as garnish) but also the roots (pounded with garlic to form a paste) and seeds (roasted, ground and used in marinades). Coriander is a good digestive aid.

LIME: The tartness of lime juice cuts through the strong, aromatic herbs and spices used in Thai dishes. Kaffir lime leaves are also a characteristic flavour in Thai cooking, imparting a sharp citrus flavour to the classic tom yum soup. Limes are much richer in vitamin C than lemons and help to reduce inflammation. The leaves can be used fresh or dried and can be stored frozen.

COCONUT MILK: Used to add sweetness to Thai curries, coconut milk is rich in saturated fat, but as it's a plant-based saturated fat it has a different fat structure to animal-based fats. This means it's readily burned as energy, rather than being stored as fat.

JAPANESE

THE JAPANESE ENJOY the longest life-expectancy in the world – despite the fact that smoking is much more popular in Japan than in the West and that they have a very high salt intake due to their consumption of seafood, soy sauce and pickled vegetables. So what is their secret? First and foremost they have an innate understanding of the influence diet has on health, meaning that they are aware of the need to choose foods for their nutritive value as much as for their taste. The Japanese diet is therefore very low in the saturated fat contained in red meat and dairy products and very rich in the healthier polyunsaturated fats of fish and seafood. Furthermore, portions of traditional Japanese dishes are much smaller than Western meals, reducing digestive strain and weight gain from over-eating.

If you're eating out at a Japanese restaurant or are cooking Japanese food at home, limit or avoid high-fat, deep-fried, battered or breadcrumbed dishes such as tempura or katsu, and don't have too much sticky rice, which is refined and very starchy, giving it a very high GL that will raise blood sugar levels. Instead, focus on the fresh fish, lean meat and vegetable options and eat slowly, savouring each of the small courses and dishes on offer, and sipping miso soup, green or jasmine tea, or even a little sake (Japanese rice wine) throughout your meal. Key Japanese superfoods include:

OILY FISH: Oily fish such as salmon or tuna feature heavily in the Japanese diet, whether it's served raw as sushi or sashimi or cooked in a sauce or soup. Eating the fish raw or lightly poached in a broth ensures that you benefit from all the skin-, heart- and brain-friendly omega 3 essential fats, which can be damaged by direct heat during cooking.

SOYA: Soya beans are a valuable part of the traditional Japanese diet. They provide protein and current thinking also attributes the low rates of breast cancer in Japan to their regular consumption. The Japanese consume soya in unadulterated forms such as miso and edamame (soya beans cooked in their pods). They do not eat the processed, additive-ridden products such as soya burgers and sausages that are becoming so popular in the West.

SOBA NOODLES: Soba noodles are made from buckwheat flour, which, despite the name, is not a form of wheat, but is gluten-free and therefore easy to digest. These noodles are ideal served in cold noodle salads or in soups, or instead of rice with a stir-fry.

SEAWEED: Seaweeds such as kombu and nori are common ingredients in Japanese dishes such as as soups and sushi. They are an excellent source of minerals such as calcium, phosphorous, magnesium, iron and iodine.

TENDERSTEM: This king of broccoli originates from Japan. It is particularly high in vitamin C and folic acid and has five times the glucosinolate content of standard broccoli. Glucosinolates aid liver detoxication enzymes and boost antioxidant status. Steam or lightly boil tenderstem in a little water to minimise any nutrient loss, or try the recipe for Soy and Sesame Steam-fried Tenderstem (see page 150).

GINGER: A characteristic flavour in Oriental cooking, ginger is delicious in broths and stir-fries, but also goes incredibly well in sweet dishes. For instance, you can add ground ginger to biscuits or granola. Rich in iron, zinc and vitamin C, as well as being antibacterial, antiviral and anti-inflammatory, ginger's health properties are renowned.

SHIITAKE MUSHROOMS: These rich, smoky-flavoured mushrooms are widely used in dishes such as stir-fries and broths. Store them in a paper bag in the fridge or buy dried. A symbol of longevity in Asia, they contain lentinan, a polysaccharide which is, in fact, an approved drug in Japan. They also contain some of the highest levels of a powerful antioxidant called ergothioneine, all eight essential amino acids and several vitamins and minerals.

CHINESE

THE CHINESE RECOGNISE that diet plays an enormous part in our health and wellbeing. Unsurprisingly, therefore, the traditional Chinese diet is generally regarded as being very healthy, featuring plenty of vegetables, fish and seafood, and very little in the way of sugar or excessively greasy foods. Like Thai food, the biggest pitfall with Chinese cuisine is the refined white rice and wheat noodles which accompany many dishes. Limit your intake to a small or medium-sized portion and focus instead on the wonderful array of stir-fried fish, meats and vegetables, as well as the broths, which will fill you up rather than fatten you. Avoid sugar-based sweet and sour sauces.

In traditional Chinese culture, cold liquids are thought to inhibit digestion, so soups and teas would be served instead of iced water or soft drinks. Teas such as green tea are believed to help in the digestion of fatty foods. Key Chinese superfoods include:

GOJI BERRIES: Native to the Himalayas, goji berries (shown opposite) are also known as wolfberries. I use them to give natural sweetness and nutrients to the Raw Chocolate and Goji Granola (see page 78) and a handful mixed with nuts also makes for a delicious and nutritious snack. Containing more beta-carotene than carrots, goji berries are also rich in vitamin C, vitamins B1 and B6, and vitamin E. They are a superb source of amino acids and minerals, including significant amounts of zinc, iron, copper and calcium, as well as essential fatty acids.

RICE: A Chinese dietary staple, in its wholegrain form – as brown rice – it is rich in fibre, potassium and B vitamins, is easily digested and has a very low allergic potential. Refined white rice is less nutritious, however; because the milling process removes the nutrient- and fibre-packed outer husks, leaving behind a starchy grain that is rapidly digested to raise blood sugar levels, without providing lasting energy.

LEMON GRASS: Lemon grass imparts a wonderful fresh, citrusy taste to spicy salads, soups and stir-fries, such as my Thai Stir-fried Beef with Chilli and Lemon Grass (see page 107). Use only the lower bulbous portion of the stem, and try pounding the stems and boiling in water to release more flavour. Since ancient times, lemon grass has been used in Chinese medicine as a digestive aid and as a tonic to relieve colds and fevers, headaches and arthritis.

GREEN TEA: Green tea is a traditional accompaniment to Chinese meals, reputed to help everything from raised cholesterol to rheumatoid arthritis. The secret behind green tea's reputation as a miracle medicine is its polyphenols, which act as powerful antioxidants and mop up free radicals before they can damage cells, as well as inhibiting the abnormal formation of blood clots.

CHICKEN: It may seem a strange choice for a superfood but it's interesting to note that the Chinese prefer dark leg meat to breast, unlike most of us in the west. It is prized for its flavour, but nutritionally it is also superior, containing two to three times as much zinc and iron as breast meat.

MIDDLE EASTERN

THE MANY DIFFERENT regions that make up the Middle East share certain culinary similarities. Grilling, frying and stewing are the most common ways of preparing meat, and spices and fresh herbs feature heavily, including garlic, cinnamon, dill, mint, parsley, coriander, cumin, oregano, turmeric, sesame seeds and pepper. In fact, the traditional Middle Eastern diet is rich in fibre from plant foods, and low in fat and cholesterol. Over time, the standard Western diet has influenced Middle Eastern eating habits, with a subsequent increase in fat, sugar and salt, but many traditional ingredients are nonetheless worth exploring for their nutritious properties as well as their flavour. Opposite are some of those superfood ingredients:

KEFIR: Similar in taste and texture to thin natural yoghurt, this fermented drink is delicious partnered with sweet fruit for a fruit salad breakfast or pudding, or blended with fruit into a smoothie. Kefir is richer in probiotic bacteria than natural yoghurt, so it helps replenish stores in the gut, aids digestion, fights infection and balances hormones. Many people who are lactose-intolerant find they have no problems with kefir as it contains enzymes that digest the lactose.

ONIONS: A regular ingredient in Middle Eastern dishes, used in everything from salads to tabouleh and tagines, onions add flavour to dishes, but also sulphurous compounds which are anti-inflammatory and antibacterial, and that help your liver detoxify harmful substances.

SESAME SEEDS: Used in breads and pastries, as a coating for stuffed dates and in sweet halva, as well as being ground to make tahini paste, sesame seeds contain a type of beneficial fibre called lignans, which have been shown to lower cholesterol and protect the liver.

POMEGRANATES: The high level of polyphenol antioxidants has given the previously obscure pomegranate A-list celebrity superfood status in recent years. Evidence suggests heart-friendly properties, with the polyphenols helping to inhibit arterial furring. The juicy, jewel-like seeds are delicious sprinkled on fruit salads such as the Morning-after Superfruit Salad (see page 80).

CHICKPEAS: Also known as garbanzos, chickpeas are a type of pulse and a common ingredient in many Middle Eastern dishes, including hummus (see page 87 for my recipe) and falafel – try my baked version on page 130. A good source of insoluble fibre to aid digestion, they are also rich in folic acid and the mineral molybdenum, which helps the body detoxify sulphites, a common preservative added to prepared foods such as deli items, dried fruit and wine.

MINT: This leafy green herb contains menthol, a compound that facilitates digestion and has antiseptic properties. A cup of sweetened mint tea is often sipped after meals or as a refreshing pick-me-up in hot weather. Rinse a sprig of fresh mint and plunge it into boiling water to make your own, unsweetened version.

LEMONS: Squeeze fresh lemon juice into cold water for a refreshing drink or drink hot water with lemon juice for a cleansing start to the day. It can also be squeezed over food such as rice or quinoa salads or plain avocado to add flavour without the need for salt. Lemons contain much more vitamin C per gram than oranges.

AFRICAN

AFRICAN COOKING STYLES vary greatly from region to region, but all focus on starchy foods and little meat, as it can be expensive and hard to come by. Local vegetables, grains and pulses are used instead for bulk and protein. North African cuisine, in particular, is growing in popularity and focuses on fresh vegetables, grains, nuts and seeds with a little meat, making it a very nutritious eating style. Dishes can vary in flavour from subtle and simple to spicy and complex, although pulse-based dishes, slow-simmered stews and charcoal-grilled meats, together with very sweet, rich pastries, feature across the regions. African cooking has also been heavily influenced by the spice trade and foreign immigrants and invaders, so Arabian flavours, such as saffron and caraway, and Indian curry spices are evident. Here are some of the key African superfoods:

DRIED FRUITS: Used to add flavour and sweetness in both sweet and savoury dishes such as tagines, dried fruit provides a concentrated source of fibre and vitamins. Apricots, especially, contain a lot of the antioxidant beta-carotene. Enjoy dried fruits sparingly, however, as they are also a concentrated source of fruit sugars and can therefore upset blood sugar levels. Choose unsulphured dried fruit as the sulphur dioxide used as a preservative has been linked to asthma and allergies.

ALMONDS: Used in sweet and savoury dishes or roasted as a snack, almonds are one of the most nutritious nuts and are rich in the antioxidant vitamin E, which helps protect the heart. They also contain magnesium, good for helping the mind and body wind down, and potassium, which is important in blood pressure control.

CUMIN: Cumin seeds provide a slightly warm, peppery flavour that is characteristic of many African dishes. Lightly roast or toast the seeds to bring out their full flavour. An excellent source of iron, which plays a key role in energy production and helps transport oxygen throughout the body, cumin is traditionally used as a digestive aid and research now shows that it may stimulate the secretion of the pancreatic enzymes that are required for digestion and the absorption of nutrients.

SWEET POTATOES: A common starchy food in African meals, sweet potatoes are actually much more nutritious than white potatoes as the orange flesh is packed with the antioxidant vitamin betacarotene as well as other vitamins and minerals. They help to stabilise blood sugar levels.

HARISSA: This highly spiced, red sauce or paste is made from chilli peppers and garlic, often with cumin, caraway and coriander, perhaps with tomatoes and olive oil. It is used both as a condiment as we might use salt and also as an ingredient in the traditional tagines of the region. Use it to marinate meat or fish (such as in the Seared Harissa Tuna Steak recipe on page 116), or stir through pasta or soup. Its high herb and spice content gives it digestive benefits.

CENTRAL AND SOUTH AMERICAN

CENTRAL AND SOUTH American dishes tend to make good use of brightly coloured local vegetables, such as red and green peppers, chillies, radishes, broccoli, tomatoes and avocados. This colour imbues the food with high levels of phytonutrients (plant nutrients). For example, tomatoes are rich in the antioxidant lycopene, which helps protect the skin from ultraviolet rays and the eyes from macular degeneration, while red onions contain quercetin, an anti-inflammatory substance that helps reduce allergy symptoms.

Maize is a commonly used carbohydrate featuring for example in corn bread or corn tortilla wraps, while pulses help to cut down the fat, increase the fibre and bulk out meat dishes such as chilli con carne. Red meat appears widely, thanks to the wide plains which are ideal for cattle grazing, and cheese is often added to dishes like fajitas and quesadillas, contributing to a fairly high overall fat intake. To avoid excess carbohydrate and saturated fat in your meal if you're eating fajitas or similar, avoid the sour cream and cheese accompaniments and simply have extra guacamole and salsa. These are some of the key superfoods of Central and South America:

AVOCADO: An avocado should be slightly soft when ripe, and a slight neck, rather than being fairly rounded, indicates that the fruit was probably ripened on the tree and will have better flavour. Avocados are rich in potassium, which helps keep blood pressure low, as well as containing oleic acid, a monounsaturated fat that may help to lower cholesterol. They are also an incredibly rich source of antioxidant carotenoids and tocopherols. The fat content in avocados helps your body absorb these carotenoids.

QUINOA: Very similar to couscous, but in fact a remarkably nutrient-dense seed rather than a grain, quinoa was once considered the 'gold of the Incas'. Today, it can be combined with herbs and vegetables to make a taboulleh-style salad or mixed with roasted Mediterranean vegetables, olives and sun-blush tomatoes. Quinoa is rare among plant foods in that it is a 'complete protein', containing all the essential amino acids that provide the body with the raw materials for growth and repair.

CACAO: The ancient Mayans and Aztecs valued the remarkable properties of the cacao bean so much that they used it as currency! Cacao is the raw unprocessed form, while conventional cocoa is the processed form of cacao. Very rich in minerals like magnesium, it is also rich and bitter in taste, so sweeten with a little agave syrup or xylitol, both of which have a low GL, to avoid raising blood sugar levels. Try it in the delicious Raw Chocolate and Goji Granola (see page 78).

YAMS: A type of sweet potato commonly used in South and Central American cooking, yams are, in fact, much sweeter than standard sweet potatoes. They also have a higher moisture content, making them suitable for not only savoury dishes, but sweet dishes such as pie fillings as well. Both yams and sweet potatoes are much richer in antioxidants than ordinary potatoes, particularly vitamin E and betacarotene.

PUMPKIN SEEDS: Sprinkle on cereal, grind into smoothies, add to flapjacks and crumbles, lightly toast, mix into salads or simply season with soy or sea salt and serve with drinks as a delicious, mineral-rich alternative to crisps. Pumpkin seeds contain both omega 3 and omega 6 essential fatty acids, making them good for the heart, skin and hormones. They are also an excellent source of zinc, which plays a big role in fertility and libido.

CARIBBEAN

CARIBBEAN COOKING STYLES vary from island to island, depending on the cosmopolitan melting pot of colonial influences and immigrants. Each relies heavily, however, on the fresh seafood, fruit and vegetables that are so abundant in this tropical paradise, as well as meat and, of course, the herbs and spices that give dishes their characteristic kick. Jerk cooking is one of the most popular forms of Caribbean cooking and it blends native food with foreign influences from Africa, Asia and Europe. Meat and fish are coated in a wet jerk paste or a dry rub and marinated for anything from a couple of hours to a couple of days before being slowly grilled, smoked or cooked in a pit. This slow-cooking method seals in flavour and preserves nutrients. Jerk flavours are highly spiced and delicious combinations of ingredients such as tamarind (see page 51), ginger (see page 55), thyme, nutmeg, onions, Scotch bonnet chillies and allspice.

The high plant intake makes the diet of the West Indies a very healthy one, rich in fibre, vitamins, minerals and phytonutrients, together with the health-giving properties of the herbs and spices, while the seafood provides lean, mineral-rich protein. Opposite are some of those key Caribbean ingredients:

COCONUT: Caribbean cooking uses coconut oil for frying, instead of the polyunsaturated vegetables oils used in the West. Because it is a saturated fat, coconut oil is able to withstand heat thus avoiding the production of harmful free radicals. This makes it the safest oil to cook with and the one which I recommend in my recipes. Furthermore, the structure of this plant-based saturated fat means that, unlike animal fats, it is used for energy rather than being stored as fat.

BANANAS: Delicious in fruit salads, smoothies or simply as a snack, bananas are rich in potassium to help lower blood pressure and dietary fibre to ease digestion. Bananas are also, however, naturally rich in fruit sugars, which will raise blood sugar levels and contribute to weight gain if eaten too often. Consequently, it's best to eat no more than one a day.

PINEAPPLES: A delicious and nutritious way to round off a meal, pineapple contains the digestive enzyme bromelain, which helps your body break down protein for easy digestion. Bromelain also has anti-inflammatory properties, helping to ease the symptoms of inflammatory conditions like asthma or allergic reactions.

WATERMELON: Its high water content makes watermelon a refreshing snack in hot weather and an excellent addition to fruit salads and smoothies. Don't pick out the seeds as these are rich in vitamin E. In studies, regular consumption of watermelon has been shown to increase blood concentrations of the antioxidants lycopene and betacarotene, as well as being excellent for skin condition.

FISH AND SEAFOOD: Best served barbecued on the beach, fish and seafood are great sources of protein, to help your body repair and rebuild itself, and zinc, to boost your libido. Oily fish such as salmon and tuna are also rich in heart- and brain-boosting omega 3 essential fats.

GARLIC: A key ingredient in jerk rub, garlic has also been used medicinally for at least 3000 years. Its allicin content makes it antibacterial and cholesterol-lowering, plus it is antiviral and anti-inflammatory, making it the ideal food when you are fighting an infection or allergic reaction. For maximum benefit, it's best eaten raw.

MEDITERRANEAN

THE MEDITERRANEAN DIET enjoys a reputation for being one of the healthiest in the world. Attention has focused particularly on the apparent paradox of its health benefits and low risk of heart disease, despite the fact that 40 per cent of its total calories come from fat. Closer inspection reveals that the types of fats which predominate in Mediterranean dishes are the healthy polyunsaturated and monounsaturated fats derived from oily fish, nuts, seeds and vegetables such as olives and avocados. These fats have been shown to have cardio-protective effects and are good sources of antioxidants, as well as helping to decrease the inflammation which is implicated in many major degenerative conditions such as diabetes, arthritis, heart disease and obesity. Furthermore, the Mediterranean diet traditionally features more fruit, vegetables, pulses, grains, garlic and herbs than the North European and American diet. These foods are, of course, high in health-giving vitamins, minerals, fibre and phytonutrients.

The Mediterranean passion for pasta, risotto and gnocchi will, however, have an effect on your waistline if you overindulge. Refined wheat and rice grains are very high in starch and low in fibre. As such, they have a high GL, which upsets blood sugar levels to leave you feeling heavy and lacking in energy, so limit your portion size and choose wholegrain versions where possible. Here are some of the key superfoods of the Mediterranean diet:

OLIVES: Rich in oleic acid, a monounsaturated fat that has been shown to lower blood cholesterol levels, olives are also a good source of vitamin E and contain phytonutrients such as polyphenols and flavonoids. These appear to have potent anti-inflammatory properties that can relieve the symptoms of conditions like asthma, eczema and arthritis.

BASIL: This fragrant herb helps digestion, so scatter a few roughly torn leaves over a salad or enjoy it in pesto. Basil also contains vitamin C and has high levels of the group of antioxidants called carotenoids, including betacarotene, which the body then converts to vitamin A.

PARSLEY: Blend large amounts of parsley with basil, watercress and a little extra virgin olive oil, sea salt and black pepper for a vivid green sauce to spread on sandwiches, swirl in soups or toss through rice, pasta and quinoa dishes. Underused as a mere garnish, this humble herb packs a mean nutritional punch and is very rich in vitamin C, calcium and betacarotene.

TOMATOES: Sun-blush or sun-dried tomatoes are delicious, distinctly Mediterranean additions to rice, quinoa or couscous salads. Cooked tomatoes (in tomato purée or canned tomatoes) are a better source of lycopene than raw tomatoes, an antioxidant shown to help protect eyesight and to boost the skin's defences against ultraviolet rays from sunlight.

FENNEL: The aniseed flavour makes it the perfect partner for fish. Fennel is also renowned for its liver-boosting abilities and is remarkably rich in vitamin C.

ARTICHOKES: Marinated artichokes in olive oil are a delicious addition to Mediterranean salads and antipasti dishes. For centuries the artichoke has been used to help detoxify the body and cleanse the blood. Today it is known to improve gall bladder secretions and boost liver function, so it's ideal if you have over-indulged in fatty foods or alcohol.

WALNUTS: Delicious sprinkled on goat's cheese salads, added to cakes or simply as a snack, walnuts are a good plant source of omega 3 fatty acids and a handful of unroasted, unsalted walnuts per day will help you to up your intake of them. In fact, nibbling on nuts has been shown to reduce risk of cardiovascular disease by anything from 15 to 50 per cent!

SHEEP'S AND GOAT'S MILK CHEESE: Sheep's cheeses, like feta and Pecorino, and goat's milk cheeses share a tangy, sharp flavour that works well in salads. The fat particles in goat's and sheep's milk are close in size to those in human breast milk and are easier to digest than cow's milk alternatives. These milks are also rich in calcium, phosphorous, zinc and B vitamins.

WESTERN

THE STANDARD WESTERN diet (i.e. that of North America, Britain and Australasia) is often vilified as the cause of all modern ills. It's certainly true that it includes far higher levels of processed foods, refined sugars and salt than traditional cuisines from the Middle East or Mediterranean. Indeed, researchers have found that a Mediterranean diet is associated with a 50 per cent lower risk of developing pulmonary diseases like bronchitis than the Western diet, even after taking into account age and smoking. It's also true that the obesity epidemic is being led by Western countries, with their proliferation of fast-food outlets and their liberal use of cheap hydrogenated fats and blood sugar-busting high fructose corn syrup.

There are, however, a wealth of nutritious foods traditionally eaten in the West. These can hold their own in the international 'superfood stakes' and they can contribute to a very healthy diet. Countries with temperate climates such as Britain benefit from a glut of delicious and wonderfully nutritious fruits and vegetables such as apples, pears, summer berries, peas and root vegetables. By focusing on whole foods and avoiding processed meals we can all enjoy a healthy diet no matter where we come from. Here are some home-grown food heroes:

OATS: Enjoy oats in porridge, muesli or granola, as well as flapjacks and crumbles. Higher in soluble fibre than all other grains, oats have an ability to lower cholesterol levels, aid healthy digestion and reduce constipation.

BARLEY: This often overlooked grain has an impressive nutritional profile as well as delicious, nutty taste and chewy consistency. Opt for pot barley, which is less refined and therefore has more nutrients than pearl barley. An excellent addition to soups and stews, and a very good alternative to rice in pilafs and risottos, barley is a good source of fibre. It provides prebiotic fuel for the good bacteria in the large intestine and is also high in beta glucans, which helps lower cholesterol.

BEETROOT: Fresh beetroot is a delicious and incredibly nutritious root vegetable that can be steamed, boiled or roasted, or even grated and eaten raw in coleslaw. Rich in soluble fibre, which can help to reduce cholesterol, it also contains iron, and antioxidant carotenoids and flavonoids, which help prevent furring of the arteries.

WATERCRESS: Use in salads or blend it on its own or with other herbs and leaves, a little extra virgin olive oil, sea salt and black pepper, for a delicious sauce to add to savoury dishes or swirl through soup. This peppery plant is incredibly rich in vitamin C, which the body

uses to produce collagen, the substance that keeps skin plump, so you could describe it as 'nature's botox'!

CRANBERRIES: These tart berries are usually sweetened in jelly as an accompaniment to turkey or drunk as a juice. Due to their proanthocyanidin content, which helps to prevent bacteria from adhering to the bladder wall, cranberries are the traditional remedy for urinary tract infections.

BLUEBERRIES: Blueberries are bursting with flavour and wonderful in fruit salads or served with pancakes, as in my Blueberry Pancakes (see page 85). Anthocyanins, the pigments which give blueberries their blue-red bloom, improve the integrity of support structures in our veins.

RASPBERRIES: Blend raspberries with banana for a rich, naturally sweet sauce for yoghurt, ice cream or muesli. They also make a great smoothie. These delicious berries are high in zinc, making them useful for skin problems, low sex drive or recurrent infections.

SUNFLOWER SEEDS: Sprinkle sunflower seeds on cereal or in flapjacks or blend into smoothies. Rich in the omega 6 essential fatty acids required for hormonal balance and soft, supple skin, sunflower seeds also contain the skin-friendly antioxidant vitamin E.

Menus

If you want inspiration for menus when entertaining, take a look at the following ideas for anything from Brunch to a Summer Lunch Party, a Low-GL Meal or a Formal Dinner Party.

Brunch

Brunch can be a great alternative to a formal sit-down meal, allowing both you and your guests to relax and munch over the morning papers while you pick and mix at a buffet. The secret to a successful brunch party is to include dishes that can be prepared the day before, particularly if you have house guests, as you are likely to come down to a kitchen full of dirty dishes and empty wine bottles from last night's supper party. I have included the delicious Raw Chocolate and Goji Granola, which is naturally sweetened with nutrient-packed goji berries (rich in B vitamins to keep you in a good mood and top up your energy levels – always needed when you're playing host or hostess) and xylitol (a natural alternative to sugar which does not upset blood sugar levels). Make things easy on yourself in the morning by preparing the granola the night before and blend up the refreshing, invigorating Blueberry and Banana Smoothie just before your guests arrive, so all you have to worry about is one dish – Smoked Salmon and Scrambled Eggs on Rye Toast – which can be made on demand or make up a big batch and dollop it out to any takers.

READY-IN-ADVANCE OPTION: Raw Chocolate and Goji Granola (see page 78)
COOKED OPTION: Smoked Salmon and Scrambled Eggs on Rye Toast (see page 81)
EASY OPTION: Blueberry and Banana Smoothie (see page 76)

Summer Lunch Party

The best summer meals are designed to showcase the fabulous flavour and freshness of seasonal food and to minimise fuss for the hot and bothered host or hostess. Where possible make use of local produce, such as fresh summer berries or asparagus, and choose dishes that can be made ahead of time. My summer lunch party menu starts with a raw dish – Feta, Watermelon and Pumpkin Seed Salad – to refresh the palette and quench thirst. Feta, a sheep's cheese, is easier to digest than cow's milk cheeses and the tart flavour works wonderfully with the sweet, juicy watermelon. To save time, this can be plated up beforehand and kept chilled. Follow it with a dish that can also be made in advance and served cold, so that you don't have to slave over a hot stove. My Wild Rice and Puy Lentils with Lemon and Asparagus is perfect. Wild rice is, in fact, not a rice grain at all, but a grass and it's much richer in protein and minerals than rice. End the meal lightly with fresh fruit, a fruit salad or a light, cool pudding such as the Pear and Coconut Cake.

STARTER: Feta, Watermelon and Pumpkin Seed Salad (see page 98)
MAIN COURSE: Wild Rice and Puy Lentils with Lemon and Asparagus (see page 137)
PUDDING: Fresh fruit, fruit salad or Pear and Coconut Cake (see page 168)

Low-GL Meal

While the vast majority of the recipes in this book are low GL, you may find it helpful to have a particularly light, low-GL menu to serve for any guests who are on a diet or are diabetic. Go for a very light starter with no heavy, starchy carbohydrates to accompany it. This will help keep the overall GL of the meal low. A salad or light soup such as Gazpacho is ideal. Follow this with a main course that features protein, such as fish, meat or pulses, rather than overloading on carbohydrates by serving a large pasta or rice dish. Eastern dishes such as stir-fries or curries are ideal choices – try my Thai Fish Cakes with soba noodles or brown basmati or low-GL rice, and Soy and Sesame Steam-fried Tenderstem. For pudding serve my low-GL Coconut and Pineapple Sorbet, a creamy but dairy-free concoction bursting with tropical flavour, along with gluten- and dairy-free Polenta Citrus Cake. This provides a sharp citrus tang to cut through any sweetness.

STARTER: Gazpacho (see page 96)
MAIN COURSE: Thai Fish Cakes (see page 124) with soba noodles or brown basmati or low-GL rice, and Soy and Sesame Steam-fried Tenderstem (see page 150)
PUDDING: Coconut and Pineapple Sorbet (see page 157) with Polenta Citrus Cake (see page 158)

Formal Dinner Party

Formal entertaining requires food with a wow factor. The following recipes should all impress your guests with their flavour and yet they won't tie you to the kitchen when you need to be looking after everyone. As for all parties, the secret to success is being prepared, so opt for a starter that can be flung together easily, like the Smoked Salmon, Dill and Avocado Platter – plate it all up in advance (on individual plates, rather than the communal platter suggested in the recipe), but add the avocado just before you serve to stop it from going brown. An old-fashioned roast with all the trimmings makes an impressive main course, so try Rosemary and Garlic Roast Lamb. I have purposefully chosen accompaniments with a lower GL than standard options such Yorkshire puddings or floury roasted potatoes, so the Roast New Potatoes recipe uses baby new potatoes as these have a lower GL. Serve with Warm Flageolet Beans with Herbs and Roasted Mediterranean Vegetables, so you fill up on fibrous, nutritious side dishes. Pudding needs to be equally impressive. The Strawberry and Banana Cheesecake and Chocolate Orange Mousse are both sure to fit the bill, but both are light enough for your guests to avoid loosening their waistbands. Home-made petits fours, such as Spelt Biscotti, make a more memorable and far healthier end to the meal than the usual box of chocolates.

STARTER: Smoked Salmon, Dill and Avocado Platter (see page 97)
MAIN COURSE: Rosemary and Garlic Roast Lamb (see page 103) with Roast New Potatoes (see page 139), Warm Flageolet Beans with Herbs (see page 148) and Roasted Mediterranean Vegetables (see page 144)
PUDDINGS: Chocolate Orange Mousse (see page 153) and Strawberry and Banana Cheesecake (see page 154) followed by a Cheese Platter (see page 156)
PETIT FOURS: Spelt Biscotti with Pistachio and Citrus (see page 160) and Chocolate Almond Apricots (see page 161)

Notes on the Recipes

As well as recipes bursting with flavoursome fresh herbs and spices and crammed with nutrient-dense fruit, whole grains, nuts and seeds, I have included plenty of gluten-, wheat- and dairy-free options, in keeping with Patrick's advice in Part One, and where possible I have suggested alternatives to make a dish suitable for special diets. For any readers abroad who struggle to get hold of some of the ingredients, you can make easy substitutions, such as using brown rice instead of quinoa or seasonal, local fruits instead of the items listed for fruit salads, for example.

Before you start cooking, the following information may be useful.

Cooking oil

I recommend frying with coconut oil or mild or medium (also known as light or second press) olive oil rather than extra virgin olive oil. This is because coconut oil and, to a lesser extent, mild or medium olive oil, sunflower and rapeseed oils are stable when heated. This means that harmful free radicals aren't produced when you cook with them. If you like the taste of more delicate oils, such as avocado or extra virgin olive oil, save them for drizzling on food once you've cooked it or for dressings, as this will preserve their flavour and their health benefits.

Coconut oil can be found in good health food stores or bought online. There are two types: extra virgin, unrefined coconut oil, which is highest in the beneficial lauric acid, and normal, non-virgin coconut oil. The extra virgin variety does have a fairly strong flavour, so some people prefer the cheaper non-virgin sort, but it is a matter of personal taste and budget.

Xylitol

You'll notice that I use xylitol as an alternative to sugar in all the sweet recipes. This naturally occurring sugar substitute is found in many plants, and has the same sweetness as sugar, but it doesn't upset blood sugar levels. In fact, you would have to eat a whopping nine spoonfuls of xylitol to have the same effect on your blood sugar levels as just one spoonful of sugar! This makes it ideal for dieters and diabetics. What's more, xylitol is naturally antibacterial, so it prevents bacteria from adhering to your teeth and helps you to avoid tooth decay – hence it appears as an ingredient in many dental products. You can find xylitol in most good supermarkets or buy it by mail order (see page 183).

Cook's Notes

Each recipe contains Cook's Notes, which provide allergy information for that particular dish. However, these refer to the ingredients in the recipe itself, not any additional serving suggestions, so this should be taken into consideration if you do have any food allergies. The Cook's Notes also tell you if the recipe can be made in advance or frozen. 'V' indicates that the recipe is suitable for vegetarians.

BRUNCH

WHETHER YOU HAVE house guests recovering from the excesses of the night before or visitors popping in, brunch is an extremely relaxing meal to enjoy with friends. It's also perfectly suited to being served buffet-style, as some people will be ready to wolf down cooked breakfasts and mountains of toast, while others will be able to face nothing more than a glass of orange juice. For this reason I recommend you pick a selection of brunch dishes to suit all appetites, including a cooked option such as Kedgeree (see page 83), a cereal such as Raw Chocolate and Goji Granola (see page 78) and a much lighter option such as the Blueberry and Banana Smoothie (overleaf). Choose a couple of dishes that can be prepared in advance and left to sit, so you only have one or two dishes such as Smoked Salmon and Scrambled Eggs on Rye Toast (see page 81) to make on demand.

Whatever you go for – and I've put together a sample menu to help (see page 70) – it's always a good idea to kick-start your metabolism with a balanced breakfast, and these delicious treats should be enough to tempt any reluctant eater into abandoning the black coffee and enjoying a proper breakfast.

BLUEBERRY AND BANANA SMOOTHIE

A smoothie is the fast track to nourishment, because the ingredients have already been broken down, meaning less work for your digestive system. This smoothie is a perfectly balanced meal in a glass, as the fruit provides energy, the berries also contain vitamins and antioxidant flavonoids, the yoghurt provides probiotics to help your digestion and boost your immunity, and the seeds contain essential fats and protein, as well as a shot of zinc.

If you make this drink in a blender, the seeds will be chopped up into small pieces that add to the texture, but if you prefer a smoother consistency, grind them in a coffee bean grinder or food processor first.

Serves 4

600g (1lb 5oz) blueberries

4 bananas

12 tbsp live natural yoghurt, kefir (see page 59)
  or soya yoghurt

4 tbsp pumpkin or sunflower seeds

a little milk, juice or water if needed

1 Blend the blueberries, bananas, yoghurt or kefir and seeds together until smooth.

2 Check the consistency and if you think it needs it, add a small amount of liquid to make the smoothie easier to drink.

Cook's Notes

Gluten-free, wheat-free, dairy-free if you use soya yoghurt • V • Can be made half an hour in advance if you add a squeeze of lemon juice to stop it from discolouring and store it in the fridge

OAT CRUNCH YOGHURT POTS

Pear and cinnamon are perfect flavour partners, but the cinnamon also serves a hidden purpose – it helps your body to regulate blood sugar levels, making this a sustaining choice that will see you through to lunch. The protein from the nuts and yoghurt is also digested more slowly than carbohydrate, ensuring a steady release of energy.

Serves 4

4 pears, cored and roughly chopped

1/2–1 tsp ground cinnamon

1 tbsp coconut oil or mild/medium (not extra virgin) olive oil

2 tbsp xylitol

50g (2oz) whole oat flakes

1 tbsp flaked almonds

1 tbsp ground almonds

1 tbsp roughly chopped macadamia nuts, hazelnuts or any other raw, unsalted nut

1 tbsp pumpkin seeds

400g (14oz) live natural yoghurt or soya yoghurt

1 Place the pears and a splash of water in a saucepan, cover and simmer for 3–5 minutes or until fairly soft. Add a little cinnamon to taste. Set aside to cool.

2 Gently heat the oil in a frying pan, then add the xylitol, oats, nuts and seeds, and stir for a couple of minutes or so to allow the oats to toast slightly. Set aside to cool.

3 Divide the stewed pears between four shallow glasses or bowls, cover with the yoghurt and top with the granola.

Cook's Notes

Wheat-free, dairy-free if you use soya yoghurt • V • Can be made in advance and stored in the fridge

RAW CHOCOLATE AND GOJI GRANOLA

Did you know that many shop-bought granolas contain as much sugar as a chocolate bar? My chewy, chocolatey granola may seem far too decadent for breakfast, but in fact it's a cunningly disguised healthy option. It is packed with seeds, to provide omega 3 and 6 essential fats which boost brain, heart and hormone function, not to mention the vitamin C and amino acid-packed goji berries. The cacao (or raw chocolate) powder adds a rich, chocolate flavour, but none of the added fat and sugar of processed chocolate. Cacao is also a good source of magnesium, nature's relaxant mineral, which will put everyone in a good mood for the rest of the day. Serve the granola with fresh berries, such as blueberries or strawberries, live natural yoghurt or even kefir (see page 59).

Serves 4

3 tbsp coconut oil or mild or medium (not extra virgin) olive oil
150g (5¹/₂oz) whole oat flakes
3 tbsp tahini
3 tbsp pumpkin seeds
3 tbsp sunflower seeds
3 tbsp sesame seeds

3 tbsp poppy seeds
3 tbsp desiccated coconut
3 tbsp goji berries
3 tbsp xylitol
1 tsp ground cinnamon
1 tsp ground ginger
3–4 tbsp cacao powder, according to taste

1 Gently heat the oil in a frying pan. Add the oat flakes, and cook for a few minutes, stirring to coat them with the oil. Then mix in the tahini for about 1 minute, spreading it around the oats fairly evenly.

2 Turn off the heat and stir in the remaining ingredients. Taste and adjust the flavour by adding more xylitol, cinnamon, ginger or cacao if necessary.

Cook's Notes
Wheat-free, dairy-free • V • Can be made in advance and stored in an airtight container in the fridge

MORNING-AFTER SUPERFRUIT SALAD

You can vary the fruit used according to your taste and the season, but the following recipe makes a fabulous summer fruit salad to top up your vitamin C levels and help cure any hangovers. The blended yoghurt and fruit make a delicious fresh smoothie for pouring over the fruit salad and along with the seeds provides protein and essential fats, which help the heart, skin, brain and hormones. This dish should be served straightaway.

Serves 4

seeds of half a pomegranate

12 handfuls strawberries, hulled and chopped

8 handfuls blueberries

2 bananas, thinly sliced

4 apricots or plums, or 2 peaches or
    nectarines, stoned and chopped

12 tbsp live natural yoghurt, kefir (see page 59)
    or soya yoghurt

8 handfuls fresh berries of your choice

a little xylitol or agave syrup to taste

4 tbsp ground or pre-cracked linseeds

2 tbsp pumpkin seeds

2 tbsp sunflower seeds

2 tbsp wheatgerm

1 Mix the pomegranate seeds, strawberries, blueberries, bananas and apricots together and divide between four bowls.

2 Blend the yoghurt or kefir with the other fresh berries and, if required, sweeten to taste with the xylitol or agave syrup.

3 Pour the blended fruit yoghurt over the fruit salad, and sprinkle the seeds and wheatgerm on top.

Cook's Notes
Gluten-free, wheat-free, dairy-free if you use soya yoghurt • V

SMOKED SALMON AND SCRAMBLED EGGS ON RYE TOAST

This is a delicious combination that makes an indulgent weekend treat, as well as providing your body with omega 3 essential fats from the salmon to nourish the heart, brain and skin, and phospholipids from the egg yolk, which are used by brain cells to aid memory. I haven't added salt to the eggs here as the smoked salmon provides extra seasoning. This is good served with raw or grilled cherry tomatoes.

Serves 4

2 tbsp coconut oil, mild or medium (not extra virgin) olive oil or butter

8 large free-range or organic eggs, beaten

4 slices rye bread

100g (4oz) smoked salmon, torn or chopped into small pieces (ideally undyed organic salmon)

freshly ground black pepper

1 Heat the oil or butter in a saucepan over a gentle heat and add the eggs. Put the bread on to toast.

2 Slowly stir the eggs with a wooden spoon, scraping along the base of the pan as they cook to keep them moving and help stop them sticking. Remove from the heat as soon as the eggs are almost set, but still a little runny as they will carry on cooking in the pan. Gently fold in the salmon pieces.

3 Put a piece of toast on each plate, and divide up the eggs and salmon. Season with black pepper.

Cook's Notes
Wheat-free if you use wheat-free rye bread, dairy-free if you use oil

COOKED BREAKFAST

The great British breakfast is not off limits to those on a health drive. A fry-up may be high in fat, but by grilling the meat and poaching the eggs you avoid adding any extra oil, and the wholemeal bread and baked beans provide fibre to help your body digest the protein from the meat and eggs. What's more, it can be adapted to suit all dietary likes and dislikes, so vegetarians can enjoy eggs and beans on toast with mushrooms and tomatoes, while meat eaters can enjoy really good quality sausages or bacon that pack a protein punch. You can also serve the eggs scrambled (see page 81) rather than poached.

Serves 4

4 good quality sausages or 8 lean slices of good quality bacon

4 tomatoes, halved and seasoned with freshly ground black pepper

2 x 400g cans baked beans

1 tbsp coconut oil, mild or medium (not extra virgin) olive oil or butter

2 handfuls of mushrooms, brushed or wiped clean then sliced

8 medium or large free-range or organic eggs

2 slices rye or wholemeal bread, toasted

1 Cook the sausages or bacon and tomatoes under the grill until the meat is cooked and the tomatoes are softened, turning halfway through.

2 Tip the baked beans into a pan, gently simmer and keep warm while you prepare the rest of the breakfast.

3 Heat the oil in a frying pan, add the mushrooms and cook for around 5 minutes or until they soften.

4 To poach the eggs, half fill a frying pan with boiling water and bring to a gentle simmer (you should just be able to see the water moving or small bubbles forming on the base of the pan). Crack the eggs into the pan, taking care not to puncture the yolk. The water should just cover them. If it doesn't, carefully add a little more boiling water. Let the eggs simmer for 4 minutes – spooning water gently over the yolks to help them to cook – before carefully lifting them out with a spatula.

5 Assemble all the elements on plates and serve.

Cook's Notes
Wheat-free if you use wheat-free rye bread, dairy-free if you use oil

KEDGEREE

This classic Scottish brunch dish is always a hit. Standard recipes slather the rice in cream and butter, but you can easily do without these high fat, digestion-straining additions. To make this a low-GL breakfast choice, my version also uses brown basmati rice, as it contains much less starch than other rice varieties, especially refined white rice, which means it releases its energy more slowly. If you can't get hold of smoked haddock you could replace it with smoked salmon or trout.

Serves 4

300g (10^1/$_2$oz) brown basmati rice or low-GL rice

1 tsp vegetable bouillon powder or salt

600g (1lb 5oz) undyed smoked haddock fillet

1 tbsp coconut oil or mild or medium (not extra virgin) olive oil

1 large onion, finely chopped

^{1}/$_2$ tsp ground turmeric

^{1}/$_2$ tsp ground coriander

^{1}/$_2$ tsp ground cumin

^{1}/$_2$ tsp hot chilli powder

100g (4oz) frozen petits pois

2 free-range or organic eggs, beaten

freshly ground black pepper

a little sea salt to taste

2 lemons, halved

1 Cook the rice according to the instructions on the pack, adding the bouillon or salt to the pan.

2 Meanwhile, poach the haddock in a pan of barely simmering water for around 4–6 minutes or until the flesh flakes easily when pressed. Carefully remove the fish from the pan and leave to cool, then remove the skin and flake into large pieces, picking out any bones that you come across.

3 Add the oil to a large saucepan and sweat the onion for a couple of minutes before adding the turmeric, coriander, cumin and chilli powder. Gently fry for another couple of minutes or so, taking care not to burn the spices, until the onions are soft and fragrant.

4 Stir the cooked rice into the spices until evenly coated, then add the frozen petits pois and cook for another few minutes to soften the petit pois. Fold in the flaked haddock.

5 Pour in the beaten egg, stirring constantly until it is cooked (this adds a glossy golden touch to the rice). Season to taste and serve immediately with a wedge of lemon.

Cook's Notes
Gluten-free, wheat-free, dairy-free

BLUEBERRY PANCAKES

This is an all-American option that I have given a makeover by using ground oats instead of refined wheat flour. This makes the pancakes easier to digest, as oats do not contain gliadin, the type of gluten that's found in wheat and that's particularly hard to digest. The blueberries are, of course, a healthier and naturally sweet alternative to adding sugar or maple syrup. This recipe makes around 25 small pancakes.

Serves 6–8

For the blueberry compote
300g (10^1/$_2$oz) blueberries
1 tbsp xylitol

For the pancakes
175g (6oz) whole oat flakes, finely blended to form a flour (using a food processor)

75g (3oz) xylitol
1 large free-range or organic egg, lightly beaten
250ml (just over 8 fl oz) milk or unsweetened non-dairy milk such as rice or soya milk
a little coconut oil or mild or medium (not extra virgin) olive oil for frying

1 Place the blueberries in a saucepan with a splash of water and leave to simmer gently for around 5–10 minutes until they soften. Sweeten them to taste with the tablespoon of xylitol and set them to one side while you make the pancakes.

2 Mix the oat flour and the 75g of xylitol in a bowl.

3 Whisk the milk into the egg to form a batter the consistency of whipping cream, then stir into the dried ingredients. If the mixture is not particularly smooth it may be that your blender isn't powerful enough to grind the oats to a fine flour. If this is the case, blend the mixture using a hand-held blender to make it as smooth as possible.

4 Heat a couple of teaspoons of oil in the base of a large frying pan and place tablespoons of the pancake mixture in the pan (without touching each other). Fry for a minute or so on each side, or until firm and golden brown. Do this in batches so as not to crowd the pan. Place the cooked pancakes on a plate and cover with a clean tea towel to keep them warm while you finish the batch.

5 Serve the pancakes covered with the blueberry compote. If you wish, top with a little yoghurt.

Cook's Notes
Wheat-free, dairy-free if you use soya milk • V • The blueberry compote can be made in advance and kept in the fridge or freezer

KIPPERS WITH RYE BREAD AND GRILLED CHERRY TOMATOES

These days kippers are rarely seen on anything other than hotel menus, but this British breakfast classic deserves to be included here, not just for its outstanding flavour, but also for its nutrient value, as kippers are a good source of omega 3 essential fats. All kippers are not equal, however, and avoid the cheap, boil-in-the-bag dyed kippers from the supermarket shelf. Instead, look at the fish counter or go to your local fishmonger to source 'proper kippers' that have been smoked – not just coated in artificial smoke flavour – and which are a deep, mahogany colour, not the lurid orange of dyed versions. You can buy ready filleted ones or fillet them yourself after cooking. If you can't get hold of kippers, you can use sardines or smoked haddock, poached for 4–6 minutes in a pan of barely simmering water until the flesh flakes easily, although the taste is not the same.

Serves 4

4 kippers

10 cherry tomatoes, ideally on the vine

4 slices of rye bread

half a lemon

freshly ground black pepper

1 Grill the kippers and tomatoes for around 5 minutes until the fish is heated through and the tomatoes start to soften.

2 Toast the bread, place a kipper on top of each slice, season with plenty of lemon juice and black pepper, and serve with the tomatoes.

Cook's Notes

Wheat-free, dairy-free

STARTERS AND LIGHT MEALS

A STARTER IS an excellent way to increase your intake of vegetables, hence the multitude of vegetable soups, salads and vegetable mezze options in this section. Starting a meal with raw vegetables via a salad such as my Greek Salad (see page 100) or a Salade Niçoise will provide your body with the necessary enzymes to help you digest the meal ahead. The majority of these recipes are meat-free, not only to allow vegetarians to enjoy them, but also to make them suitably light, balanced starters when served before a main course from the meat or fish section.

HUMMUS

Hummus is a classic Middle Eastern staple that is rich in fibre and antioxidants from the garlic, tahini and lemon juice. I have managed to cut down on the oil and salt content compared to standard versions without compromising on flavour. As a starter with crudités, this recipe serves four, but with the addition of some wholemeal pitta bread it would make a main meal for two.

Serves 4

410g can chickpeas in water, rinsed and drained, or 240g (just under 9oz) dried chickpeas, cooked

juice of half a lemon

1 large garlic clove, crushed

1 tbsp tahini

75ml (2½fl oz) extra virgin olive oil

1 tsp sea salt to taste

1 Blend all the ingredients together until smooth and creamy. If you want a smoother consistency, add an extra drizzle of olive oil or a splash of water.

2 Taste and adjust seasoning if required.

Cook's Notes
Gluten-free, wheat-free, dairy-free, yeast-free • V • Can be made in advance and keeps up to five days in the fridge

ROASTED BUTTERNUT SQUASH WEDGES WITH SPICY DIPPING SAUCE

The mild, sweet roasted squash is enlivened here by an Oriental-style dipping sauce bursting with the flavours of fresh ginger, coriander, sesame and spring onions. This recipe came about by happy accident when I was polishing off some leftovers after testing the recipe for Indian Spiced Butternut Squash (see page 141) and the sauce for the Salmon with Ginger Sauce (seee page 123). The result is delicious finger food, which is perfect for part of a mezze selection to share with friends.

Serves 4

For the squash wedges

950g (2lb 2oz) butternut squash, unpeeled

1 tbsp mild or medium (not extra virgin) olive oil

For the sauce

2 tbsp root ginger, peeled

10 spring onions, topped, tailed and halved

1 tbsp fresh coriander

3 tbsp tamari or soy sauce

3 tbsp toasted sesame oil

3 tbsp water

juice of 2 limes or lemons

freshly ground black pepper

salt

1 Preheat the oven to 200°C/400°F/gas mark 6.

2 Cut the butternut squash in half lengthways and scrape out the seeds and pulp with a spoon. Cut again lengthways into eighths, so you have eight long strips in total.

3 Rub the oil all over the squash then place in a roasting dish and cook for around 45–60 minutes until the flesh is soft when pierced or squashed, removing from the oven halfway through to turn the pieces over.

4 While the squash is cooking, make the dipping sauce. Whizz the ginger, spring onions, coriander, tamari or soy, sesame oil, water and lime or lemon juice together in a blender until it forms a relatively smooth sauce and the ginger is finely chopped. Taste and adjust the seasoning.

5 Arrange the squash on a platter with a bowl of the dipping sauce and encourage everyone to dip in.

Cook's Notes

Gluten-free, wheat-free if you use tamari, dairy-free • V • Can be made in advance

VEGETABLE ANTIPASTI MEZZE

This is the perfect summer starter. Simply choose any or all of the following antipasti ideas and let people serve themselves. If you don't have the time or inclination to make your own hummus or guacamole, you can buy them from the supermarket or deli, but go for good quality versions that are free from artifical preservatives and flavours. The bright colours of the vegetables show their phytonutrient and antioxidant content, which will help keep your guests healthy, but there is also plenty of fibre in the vegetables, chickpeas and whole grains to aid digestion. To turn this into a main meal, you could serve it with the Cashew and Herb Corn Bread (see page 140).

Serves 4

For the guacamole
4 avocados
juice of 1 lemon
1 red onion, finely diced
1 mild red chilli, deseeded and finely chopped
2 garlic cloves, crushed
1/2 bunch coriander, finely chopped
1/2 bunch flat leaf parsley, finely chopped
freshly ground black pepper

4 wholemeal pitta breads, griddled and cut into diagonal strips
bag of mixed leaves, 2 Little Gems or a Romaine lettuce, washed and roughly torn
jar of olives
jar of marinated artichoke hearts, sun-dried peppers or sun-blush tomatoes
4 servings of Hummus (see page 87)
2 servings of Greek Salad (see page 100)
4 servings of Marinated Griddled Courgettes (see page 145)

1 To make the guacamole, mash the avocados with the lemon juice, onion, chilli, garlic, coriander and parsley. Add the freshly ground black pepper to taste.

2 Arrange the guacamole and all the other mezze choices on a large platter or in bowls in the middle of the table and let people help themselves.

Cook's Notes
Dairy-free if you don't have the Greek Salad • V • Can be made in advance

HOT SMOKED SALMON WITH MANGO SALSA

This delicious, light starter was inspired by a similar recipe served by my friends Colin and Alex Orr at a dinner party. A doddle to make, this dish can be plated up in advance so that you focus on the main course or on enjoying your party. Hot-smoked fish is smoked directly over a fire, whereas cold smoking uses the smoke alone, which doesn't kill any microbes present. If you can't find hot-smoked salmon you can easily substitute cold smoked fish. The salmon provides a healthy dose of omega 3 essential fats, while the mango's orange flesh contains the antioxidant vitamin betacarotene and the avocado is packed with skin-healing vitamin E.

Serves 4

1 large ripe mango

1 ripe avocado

1/2 mild red chilli, deseeded and finely chopped

4 spring onions, finely sliced

juice of 1 lime

zest of 1 lime, finely grated

25g (1oz) coriander, finely chopped

2 hot-smoked salmon fillets, cut in half lengthways to produce 4 slim fillets

4 small handfuls of rocket, lamb's leaf lettuce or mixed leaves

freshly ground black pepper

1 Slice the mango flesh off both sides of the stone, scoring the flesh lengthways and then horizontally to produce small cubes. Over a bowl so that you capture the juice, scrape the cubes from the skin using a spoon.

2 Stir in all the remaining ingredients, except for the fish, leaves and pepper, and mix well.

3 Place a salmon fillet and spoonful of salsa on each plate. Add the leaves and season with black pepper.

Cook's Notes
Gluten-free, wheat-free, dairy-free • Can be made in advance

THAI STEAMED PRAWN POTS

Prawns, like all shellfish, are a good source of lean protein. Here their flavour is greatly enlivened by the addition of Thai spices, which will also help the body to digest this and any further courses. For this dish you will need four ramekins that hold around 100ml (just over 3fl oz) each.

Serves 4

300g (10^1/$_2$oz) raw prawns, shelled and
  deveined
2 heaped tbsp coconut cream
2 tsp Thai red curry paste
1 tbsp nam pla or Thai fish sauce
2 pinches of xylitol
1 small mild red chilli, deseeded

2cm/1in chunk of root ginger, roughly chopped
1 large free-range or organic egg
4 tbsp raw unsalted cashew nuts, lightly
  toasted in a dry frying pan
1 tbsp fresh coriander
drizzle of toasted sesame oil

1 Cut out four circles of baking paper to cover each ramekin.

2 Place the prawns, coconut cream, curry paste, nam pla, xylitol, chilli, ginger, egg and half the cashew nuts in a blender and whizz to form a rough paste.

3 Divide the paste evenly between the ramekins and place a baking paper circle on top of each one.

4 Arrange the ramekins in a steamer pan or machine. They should all be on the same level to ensure that they cook evenly, which may mean cooking them in two batches. Cover and steam them for around 12 minutes or until the prawn paste feels firm to the touch and the middle is cooked (pierce one with a knife to check). Remove the paper topping when cooked.

5 Meanwhile, roughly chop the remaining cashew nuts and the coriander and scatter over the prawn pots. Before serving, drizzle each one with a little sesame oil.

Cook's Notes
Gluten-free, wheat-free, dairy-free

CHICKEN SATAY SKEWERS

This Eastern-style satay sauce is packed with healthy ingredients from the ginger, garlic and onion to the chilli, lemon and coriander, all of which can help your body to fight infections. You will need skewers for this recipe. Metal ones save time as they don't need soaking, whereas wooden ones need soaking in water for 30 minutes to prevent them from burning. The wooden ones are, however, much easier to pick up and turn when hot.

Serves 4

For the sauce

4 tbsp peanuts or cashew nuts, lightly toasted in a dry frying pan and finely chopped

4 tbsp sugar-free crunchy peanut butter

2 tbsp groundnut oil or untoasted sesame oil

2 tbsp water

2 garlic cloves, crushed

2 heaped tbsp root ginger, peeled and grated

1 tbsp finely chopped mild red chilli

3 heaped tbsp finely chopped fresh coriander

4 spring onions, very finely sliced

1–2 tsp tamari or soy sauce

2–3 tbsp toasted sesame oil

juice of 1 lemon or 2 limes

For the chicken

500g (1lb 2oz) skinless, boneless chicken thigh fillets, cut into bite-sized pieces

2 tbsp medium or mild (not extra virgin) olive oil

1 tbsp tamari or soy sauce

1 If you're using wooden skewers, soak them for 30 minutes in water.

2 Make the satay sauce by stirring all the ingredients, except the toasted sesame oil and lemon or lime juice, together. Alternatively, if you want to save time on the chopping and grating, whizz the ingredients together in a blender. Then add the reserved oil and juice little by little, testing for consistency and taste. Spoon the sauce into a small bowl.

3 Preheat the grill to a high heat. Place the chicken in a bowl, drizzle with the oil and tamari or soy and mix to coat. Thread the chicken onto the skewers.

4 Grill the chicken for around 10 minutes, turning occasionally so that it cooks evenly, until the meat is cooked through and the juices run clear. Divide the skewers between four plates and invite guests to help themselves to the sauce.

Cook's Notes

Gluten-free, wheat-free if you use tamari, dairy-free • The sauce can be made in advance and the skewers can be prepared and then chilled until you're ready to grill them

PESTO MUSHROOMS ON GRILLED POLENTA SLICES

When it comes to the pesto in this dish, it's worth paying a little more for 'proper' pesto, as the cheaper brands and reduced-fat versions seem to contain a lot of unwanted fillers and additives such as starches and milk proteins. You can buy pre-cooked blocks of polenta, which is cooked corn meal, in most supermarkets and delis, and it makes a very easy, instant base for a starter or light meal such as this new take on a toasted bruschetta. Corn is also gluten- and gliadin-free, which makes it easy to digest and suitable for anyone suffering from IBS or coeliac disease.

Serves 4

500g (1lb 2oz) block of pre-cooked polenta, sliced into 8

1 tbsp mild or medium (not extra virgin) olive oil

450g (1lb) mushrooms, sliced

4–5 tbsp pesto

freshly ground black pepper

handful of fresh basil leaves, roughly torn

1 Preheat a grill to a medium-high heat and grill the polenta slices for around 5–8 minutes, turning halfway through, until each side starts to crispen and turn golden. You may have to do this in batches.

2 Meanwhile, heat the oil in a frying pan and sauté the mushrooms gently for a few minutes until cooked.

3 Stir the pesto into the mushrooms and then spoon the mixture onto the grilled polenta slices.

4 Sprinkle with black pepper and basil leaves before serving.

Cook's Notes
Gluten-free, wheat-free • V

CHICKPEA, CARROT AND CORIANDER SOUP

This recipe was inspired by a delicious soup I ate at a little restaurant called Pickwicks, in the sleepy Dorset town of Beaminster, which serves a different, freshly made, seasonal soup each day. When I asked for the recipe, the chef was hard-pressed to give it to me, as he simply cooks by eye, but this is my recreation of it. Grating the carrots means that they soften very quickly – reducing the cooking time and therefore reducing any loss of nutrients. Serve this soup on its own or with some crusty wholemeal, seeded or granary rolls, or soda bread.

Serves 4

410g can chickpeas

1 tbsp coconut oil, mild or medium (not extra virgin) olive oil or butter

1 white onion, finely sliced

4 medium carrots, thickly grated

800ml (just under 2pt) hot vegetable stock

80g (just over 3oz) coriander, flat leaf parsley or a mix of the two

1 tbsp extra virgin olive oil

2 tbsp lemon juice

freshly ground black pepper

1 Drain and rinse the chickpeas, and then blend them until smooth. If necessary, add a splash of water to get a puréed consistency.

2 Heat the oil or butter in a large saucepan and gently sweat the onion for around 5 minutes to soften it.

3 Stir in the carrots then pour in the vegetable stock and bring to the boil. Cover and simmer for 10 minutes, or until the carrot tastes soft and a little sweet rather than coarse and raw, stirring in the puréed chickpeas halfway through.

4 Meanwhile, place the herbs, oil and lemon juice in a blender or food processor and blitz until the herbs are finely chopped and fairly smooth.

5 Ladle the soup into bowls and place a dollop of the herb garnish in the middle before sprinkling with black pepper.

Cook's Notes
Gluten-free, wheat-free, dairy-free • V • Can be made in advance, but add the garnish before serving • The soup, but not the herb garnish, is suitable for freezing

GAZPACHO

A bowlful of this Spanish soup makes a refreshing alternative to a salad as a light summer lunch or starter. In addition to tomatoes, which provide plenty of lycopene, the antioxidant known to mop up free radicals from ultraviolet rays before they can damage skin and cause wrinkles, my version contains a mixture of raw vegetables for extra flavour and nutrients. Gazpacho is traditionally served chilled, so you could pop it in the fridge for 30 minutes to an hour before serving, but it is also perfectly delicious eaten straight after it is made.

Serves 4

3 red, yellow or orange peppers or a mixture
   of colours, deseeded

1 cucumber

1 red onion

3 sticks of celery

400g (14oz) ripe tomatoes

2 garlic cloves, crushed

2 mild red chillies, deseeded

125g (4¹/₂oz) Peppadew sweet baby peppers,
   drained weight, or hot pepper or chilli sauce
   to taste

2 handfuls of coriander

2 handfuls of flat leaf parsley

2 ripe avocados

400ml (just over 13fl oz) tomato juice

juice of 2 lemons

freshly ground black pepper

sea salt

1 Place the peppers, cucumber, onion, celery, tomatoes, garlic, chillies, Peppadew peppers, coriander and flat leaf parsley in a food processor and process to chop finely.

2 Halve and de-stone the avocados, then dice the flesh and add it to the soup mixture, along with the tomato juice, lemon juice, black pepper and salt. Stir together and adjust the seasoning to taste. If you prefer a milder flavour, don't add the Peppadew peppers or sauce and double the amount of avocado.

Cook's Notes
Gluten-free, wheat-free, dairy-free • V • Can be made in advance and chilled

SMOKED SALMON, DILL AND AVOCADO PLATTER

This is an incredibly simple dish to make and one which really shows off the fabulous flavours of the ingredients. Salmon is, of course, rich in omega 3 essential fats to help the brain, heart, skin and hormones, while avocado is rich in heart-friendly monounsaturated fats and the antioxidant vitamin E. Served with triangles of toasted pumpernickel-style rye bread, this dish makes a lovely, light summer starter.

Serves 4

250g (9oz) smoked salmon, roughly torn into strips

2 ripe avocados

juice of 1 lemon

2 tbsp finely chopped fresh dill

freshly ground black pepper

1 Lie the smoked salmon out on a large platter or individual plates.

2 Halve and stone the avocados, slice the flesh, taking care not to cut through the skin, and scoop it out of the skin with a spoon.

3 Scatter the avocado slices over the salmon. Squeeze lemon juice over the top and sprinkle with the dill and lots of black pepper.

Cook's Notes

Gluten-free, wheat-free, dairy-free, yeast-free

FETA, WATERMELON AND PUMPKIN SEED SALAD

This unusual but delicious salad combination makes brilliant finger food to serve at a buffet or barbecue as a shared starter, but you could also plate it individually and serve it on a bed of spinach, watercress and rocket. Watermelon is rich in lycopene and its seeds contain the antioxidant vitamin E for healthy skin. You can use up the leftover watermelon by making the Watermelon Whiz drink (see page 176) or add it to smoothies or fruit salads.

Serves 4

4 tbsp pumpkin seeds

half a watermelon, rind removed, sliced into
    thinnish wedges

200g (7oz) feta cheese

4 tbsp black olives, pitted and halved

freshly ground black pepper

1 Lightly toast the pumpkin seeds in a dry frying pan for a few minutes until they start to pop. Leave to cool.

2 Place the watermelon wedges on a large platter.

3 Crumble the feta cheese over the top and sprinkle with the olives and pumpkin seeds. Season with black pepper.

Cook's Notes
Gluten-free, wheat-free • V • Can be made in advance, but keep it chilled

GREEK SALAD

In my opinion, this classic is one of the most flavour-packed and delicious salads ever created. It is also bursting with vitamins, enzymes and antioxidants from the fresh, raw vegetables, plus it provides a range of different phytonutrients from the different coloured vegetables. Feta is a sheep's milk cheese, which is easier to digest than cow's milk products and is less likely to cause allergies and intolerances. You could serve the salad with toasted wholemeal pitta bread to make this a more substantial lunch.

Serves 4

250g (9oz) cherry tomatoes, halved

1 large red onion, diced

1 cucumber, quartered lengthways and sliced into triangular chunks

100g (4oz) Kalamata olives, pitted

juice of half a lemon

2 tsp dried oregano

freshly ground black pepper

200g (7oz) feta cheese, cut into small chunks

1 Stir all the ingredients, except the feta, together in a bowl.

2 Mix in the feta, but do it gently, as too much mixing can turn the rest of the salad a milky colour, which loses the effect of the vibrant colours.

Cook's Notes

Gluten-free, wheat-free • V

MEAT AND POULTRY MAIN COURSES

MEAT OFTEN GETS a bad press. Its reputation has suffered over the last few years due to the fad for low-fat diets and increasing concerns over obesity and heart disease. In fact, red meat, such as beef or pork, can be just as lean, if not leaner, than white meat such as poultry. It all depends on the cut of meat and the animal itself. Yes, red meat is naturally fattier than white meat but intensively reared chickens that are kept cheek to jowl with no room to exercise have been shown to have 25 per cent more fat than organic birds, which is enough to rival any beef steak or pork chop.

Fat does of course contribute flavour and texture to cooked meat but it is not just the increase in the amount of fat in animals that is the problem, but the type of fat itself. Due to changes in farming methods the ratio of polyunsaturated fats to saturated fats in intensively farmed animals is now 1:50. In organically or traditionally reared animals, which have a more natural diet and lifestyle, the ratio is 1:2.

Polyunsaturated fats include the essential fat omega 3, which is used for essential functions within the body rather than being stored as fat and is known to be beneficial for heart health. A 2002 study found that organic chickens contained 38 per cent more omega 3 fat than their intensively farmed cousins. It also observed that the organic chicken's ability to roam freely reduced abdominal fat by a massive 65 per cent. In taste tests, the organic birds also scored significantly higher for juiciness. Intensively produced meat, be it chicken or beef, is likely, therefore, to have a much higher proportion of saturated fat. As saturated fat is readily stored as fat, is hard to digest, contributes to constipation and increases inflammation in the body, which in turn has been linked to chronic degenerative diseases, this situation is hardly ideal.

I am by no means, however, advocating vegetarianism for all and in fact I'm a firm meat-eater. Indeed certain constitutional types require and indeed thrive on a high meat intake, and meat is, of course, a valuable source of nutrients, such as zinc, vitamin A and protein.

It would seem prudent, though, to choose better quality meat from organically or traditionally reared animals and to balance your meat intake with other sources of protein, such as fish, eggs, nuts, seeds, beans and pulses, all of which are lower in saturated fat.

Meat should also, in my opinion, always be accompanied by some form of fibre to aid in digestion, so opt for a salad alongside your steak or roasted vegetables with your roast. The recipes here are all well balanced in this regard, as well as featuring a range of leaner types of meat, such as venison, which is naturally very low in fat, or pork loin, rather than fatty pork belly or chops.

In addition, it is not just saturated fat that we need to be mindful of when choosing meat. Intensively farmed animals are routinely exposed to antibiotics to avoid or treat disease, or as growth promoters, and this gives rise to antibiotic-resistant bacteria. Residues from antibiotics remain in intensively reared meat and are passed on to us when we eat it, transferring the antibiotic resistance to us, so our health, just like that of the animal, is likely to be compromised. Organic livestock farmers manage their animals without the routine use of antibiotics and other drugs. Animals are fed good quality organic feed and they are not overcrowded, which is an important factor in the spread of disease.

Knowing this, it is fairly hard to justify intensive livestock farming. The only thing in its favour is, of course, cost, but this so-called 'value' supermarket meat comes at a high price, when quality, our own health and that of the animal suffers. If cost prevents you from buying better quality meat, then you may wish to consider reducing the amount of meat that you and your family eat, so that you can afford to spend a little more on a better quality product, even if you don't have meat so often. Some fish, plus eggs, nuts, seeds, beans and pulses are in general much more economical sources of protein and are extremely nutritious in their own right. If you reduce the amount of meat you eat and eat more of these alternatives, your diet will also become more balanced. There are plenty of well balanced vegetarian choices in this book to give you some ideas.

ROSEMARY AND GARLIC ROAST LAMB

This is a classic combination that never fails to please. The French often partner lamb with pale, delicately flavoured and textured flageolet beans, and I recommend you serve this dish with the Warm Flageolet Beans with Herbs, Roasted Mediterranean Vegetables (see page 144) and Roast New Potatoes (see page 139). All these vegetables will provide fibre to help make the meat easier to digest.

Serves 4–6

2 tbsp mild or medium (not extra virgin) olive oil

4 large garlic cloves, crushed

2 good pinches of sea salt

1 tbsp rosemary, finely chopped

2kg (4lb 6oz) leg of lamb

1 Preheat the oven to 190°C/375°F/gas mark 5.

2 Mix together all the ingredients except the meat and rub the resulting paste over the lamb.

3 Place the lamb in a roasting tin and cook for 30 minutes. Then reduce the oven temperature to 170°C/325°F/gas mark 3 and cook for another hour and a half (25 minutes per 450g/1lb of meat). Baste and turn the joint every 30 minutes or so and turn the leg over twice to ensure that it cooks evenly.

4 Remove the lamb from the oven, wrap it in tin foil and allow it to rest on a carving board for 25 minutes before serving.

Cook's Notes

Gluten-free, wheat-free, dairy-free, yeast-free

BRAISED LAMB SHANKS WITH FLAGEOLET BEANS

Serve with mashed sweet potato or normal potato (try Vivaldi potatoes – they have such a wonderfully creamy consistency when mashed that there's no need to add butter or milk). Leave the skins on the potato for added fibre and texture.

Serves 4

2 tbsp mild or medium (not extra virgin) olive oil

4 x 450g (1lb) lamb shanks, trimmed of excess fat and skin where possible

1/2 bottle of full-bodied red wine

570ml (1pt) lamb stock or half chicken, half beef

1 garlic clove, sliced

300g (10 1/2oz) shallots, peeled

1 carrot, thinly sliced

1 stick of celery, thinly sliced

325g (just under 11 1/2oz) butternut squash, unpeeled, seeds removed and cubed

1 bay leaf

1 sprig of fresh thyme

410g can flageolet beans, rinsed and drained, or 240g (just under 9oz) dried weight flageolet beans, cooked

1 tbsp cornflour, mixed with 2 tbsp cold water

freshly ground black pepper

1 Preheat the oven to 170°C/325°F/gas mark 3. Heat a tablespoon of the oil in a large frying pan and brown the shanks, one or two at a time, on all sides, adding more oil to the pan if necessary. Transfer the shanks to a large casserole dish.

2 Add the wine to the pan and scrape the base to remove any sediment before adding the stock, garlic, shallots, carrot, celery, butternut squash, bay leaf and thyme. Boil for a couple of minutes.

3 Transfer to the casserole dish and place in the oven to cook for two and a half hours or until the meat comes away from the bone easily. Turn off the oven, remove the shanks and place them in a covered dish. Put them back in the oven to keep warm.

4 Put the casserole dish, which still contains the cooking liquid, on the hob (make sure the dish won't crack if you do this). Add the flageolet beans and slaked cornflour and boil, uncovered, for a further 20 minutes or so to thicken the sauce. Pour the sauce over the shanks to serve.

Cook's Notes
Gluten-free, wheat-free if you use a wheat-free stock, dairy-free, yeast-free • Can be made in advance • Suitable for freezing

VENISON SAUSAGES BRAISED WITH RED WINE, ROSEMARY AND SAGE

Venison sausages can now be found in good supermarkets or, even better, at farmers' markets or direct from the producers, which usually means a better quality product. Venison is one of the leanest meats and is a very rich source of B vitamins, iron and phosphorus. As it isn't intensively reared, venison also avoids the problems of antibiotic residues. Serve with mashed or baked sweet potato to help mop up the rich sauce and some shredded and steamed Savoy cabbage or spring greens.

Serves 4

2 tbsp coconut oil or mild or medium (not extra virgin) olive oil

12 venison sausages

4 large garlic cloves, peeled

500g (1lb 2oz) shallots, peeled

6 sticks of celery, thickly sliced on the diagonal

400g (14oz) chestnut mushrooms, quartered

420ml (14fl oz) hot beef stock

600ml (1pt) good quality red wine

4 carrots, sliced

2 tbsp rosemary leaves, chopped

2 tbsp sage leaves, chopped

1–2 tbsp cornflour mixed with 2–4 tbsp cold water until smooth

freshly ground black pepper

sea salt to taste

1 Heat the oil in a casserole dish or large frying pan, add the sausages and brown for 8–10 minutes until they are evenly coloured all over. Do this in batches if necessary. Transfer to a plate.

2 Sweat the garlic, shallots, celery and mushrooms in the same pan for 5 minutes.

3 Return the sausages to the pan, along with the beef stock, red wine, carrots, rosemary and sage. Bring to the boil and simmer very gently, covered, for around 30 minutes, then remove the lid and simmer uncovered for another 20 minutes or so to reduce the liquid.

4 Add the cornflour and water mixture to the pan to thicken the liquid, stirring for a couple of minutes as it comes to the boil and thickens the sauce. Season with pepper and taste. Add salt if needed.

Cook's Notes

Gluten-free, wheat-free, dairy-free depending on the contents of the sausages • Can be made in advance

THAI STIR-FRIED BEEF WITH CHILLI AND LEMON GRASS

This stir-fry sauce is rich in flavour and nutrients – from the digestion-boosting chilli and lemon grass to the anti-inflammatory ginger and garlic. Serve with stir-fried vegetables and glass (mung bean) noodles if you can get hold of them (look in Chinese supermarkets). Otherwise, serve with brown rice noodles or soba (buckwheat – gluten-free, despite the name) noodles, or low-GL or brown basmati rice.

Serves 4

For the sauce

1 1/2 lemon grass stems

1 tsp mild red chilli, deseeded

2.5cm (1in) chunk root ginger, peeled

3 medium garlic cloves

1/2 tbsp tamarind paste

1 tbsp coconut oil or mild or medium (not extra virgin) olive oil

600g (1lb 5oz) good quality steak, cut into strips

2 tbsp nam pla or Thai fish sauce

1 tbsp fresh lime juice

1 Remove the tough outer layers from the lemon grass and soak the soft inner core in boiling water for 5 minutes to get maximum flavour.

2 Blend the lemon grass and other sauce ingredients together until well combined.

3 Heat the oil in a wok or large frying pan until very hot, then add the beef and the blended sauce. Cook on a high heat for a minute or so, until the meat is seared.

4 Add the fish sauce and lime juice, stir and serve.

Cook's Notes

Gluten-free, wheat-free, dairy-free

GREEK-STYLE STUFFED PORK TENDERLOIN

Serve this full-flavoured pork dish with Peperonata (see page 146) or a mixed salad or steamed vegetables and new potatoes. Parma ham may be quite fatty, but its fat content will help to keep the very lean tenderloin moist when cooking and hold the juices in.

Serves 4

2 x 400g (14oz) pork tenderloin fillets
150g (just over 5oz) soft goat's cheese
100g (4oz) sun-blush or sun-dried tomatoes,
 roughly chopped

2 tsp dried oregano
4 stalks of thyme
freshly ground black pepper
12 slices Parma ham

1 Preheat the oven to 190°C/375°F/gas mark 5.

2 Slice along the length of each piece of tenderloin, through the middle without cutting it into two pieces, so that you can splay the meat out and stuff the middle.

3 Prepare the stuffing by mashing the goat's cheese, tomatoes, oregano, thyme and pepper together with a fork. Spread the mixture along the middle of the opened-out tenderloin. Roll or fold the tenderloins back together.

4 Carefully wrap 3 slices of Parma ham around each tenderloin to seal it. You could tie string around the loins at this stage to help prevent the juices from escaping during cooking, but this is not essential.

5 Place the pork on a baking tray, cover with tin foil then bake for 10 minutes. Uncover and return to the oven for a further 20 minutes, until the pork is cooked through and the ham is crispy.

6 Cover the meat in tin foil and leave it to rest for 5 minutes, to tenderise it. If you're using string, remove it and cut the pork into medallions or thick slices.

Cook's Notes
Gluten-free, wheat-free • Can be prepared in advance

SMOKED PAPRIKA CHICKEN

These drumsticks make perfect barbecue or buffet food as it's almost inevitable you will end up eating them with your fingers. Please make sure you use smoked paprika for the marinade. It's easy to find in supermarkets and delis, and it has a much better flavour than the ordinary variety. Also, don't worry that this recipe seems to call for a lot of salt – much of it will be left behind in the marinade bowl. Did you know that the dark meat found in chicken thighs contains more minerals, such as iron and zinc, than the white meat found in chicken breasts? You can leave the skin if you wish – it does taste fabulous and if you buy organic meat you'll avoid many of the problems associated with eating animal fat, which is where toxins are stored. These moreish drumsticks are good served with a baked potato or sweet potato, or the Cashew and Herb Corn Bread (see page 140), together with salad and coleslaw.

Serves 4

4 tbsp mild or medium (not extra virgin) olive oil

4 tsp smoked paprika

4 tsp sea salt

8 large or 12 small chicken drumsticks, skin on

1 Mix the oil, paprika and salt together in a mixing bowl and rub this marinade over the chicken drumsticks. Push back the skin to coat the flesh itself, then pull the skin back to cover the flesh and stop it from drying out under the grill.

2 When all the drumsticks are well coated, cover the bowl and put in the fridge for about an hour. This helps to tenderise the meat and impart more flavour, but it's not a disaster if you have less time or skip this step completely.

3 Preheat the grill to medium-high and grill the drumsticks for 20 minutes, or until the flesh is no longer pink and the juices run clear. Turn them every 5 minutes or so to colour them on all sides. Towards the end of the cooking period you can turn the heat up to high, to crisp up the skin slightly, but monitor them closely to make sure they don't burn. These drumsticks can be served hot or cold, but the flesh will be more tender when they're still hot from the grill.

Cook's Notes

Gluten-free, wheat-free, dairy-free, yeast-free • Can be made in advance

CHICKEN BREASTS STUFFED WITH OLIVES, SAGE AND WALNUTS

The strong flavour of fresh sage is a good partner for the olives, while the walnuts add healthy polyunsaturated fats and minerals. To save space and time, you can also put some chopped vegetables into the roasting tin to cook alongside the chicken. Start cooking them 30 minutes before you add the chicken and follow the instructions for Roasted Mediterranean Vegetables (see page 144). Add diced sweet potatoes or butternut squash to the usual medley of red onions, peppers and courgettes to provide slow-releasing carbohydrate or serve with Roast New Potatoes (see page 139) and steamed vegetables or salad.

Serves 4

4 organic or free-range chicken breasts, skinless and boneless
150g (5^1/$_2$oz) Kalamata olives, pitted
1 garlic clove
15g (^{1}/$_2$ oz) fresh sage leaves

100g (4oz) walnut halves
4 tbsp mild or medium (not extra virgin) olive oil plus a little extra
freshly ground black pepper

1 Preheat the oven to 180°C/350°F/gas mark 4. Rub a little oil over the base of a roasting tin.

2 Carefully cut a slit in the side of each chicken breast to create a pocket.

3 Blend, or finely chop and mix together, the olives, garlic, sage, walnuts and oil until fairly smooth.

4 Stuff each chicken breast with the olive mixture. Rub the excess over the top of each chicken breast and place them in the roasting tin.

5 Put the roasting tin on a baking tray and cook for around 20–25 minutes or until the meat juices run clear. Sprinkle with black pepper before serving.

Cook's Notes
Gluten-free, wheat-free, dairy-free • Can be made in advance – the chicken can be stuffed and kept in the fridge or cooked and served cold

MOROCCAN-STYLE CHICKEN

This is a warming, mildly spiced casserole with melt-in-the-mouth braised butternut squash. However, the spices impart health benefits as well as flavour. The cinnamon, for example, helps your body regulate blood sugar levels, while turmeric is a potent anti-inflammatory. Serve with quinoa for a gluten-free alternative to couscous or low-GL or brown basmati rice, accompanied by steamed broccoli or tenderstem.

Serves 4

1 tbsp coconut oil or mild or medium (not extra virgin) olive oil

2 red onions, sliced

4 organic or free-range chicken breasts, skin and fat removed, cubed

700g (1lb 11oz) butternut squash, unpeeled, seeds scraped out and cubed

1 tsp ground cinnamon

1 tsp ground ginger

1 tsp turmeric

1L (35fl oz) chicken stock

fresh coriander and mint for sprinkling

freshly ground black pepper

1 Heat the oil in a large saucepan and sweat the onion for 3–4 minutes, then add the chicken, squash and spices, and stir for another couple of minutes.

2 Pour in the stock, bring to the boil, then cover and simmer for 30 minutes. Uncover and simmer for a further 10 minutes to allow the meat to cook fully (the juices should run clear) and the sauce to thicken. Sprinkle with coriander, mint and black pepper before serving.

Cook's Notes
Gluten-free, wheat-free, dairy-free • Can be made in advance

FISH

MANY PEOPLE DISMISS fish as difficult to prepare or cook, but I have come up with some incredibly simple, quick and foolproof fish recipes that enable you to offer light dishes that are lower in fat and, in the case of the oily fish dishes such as the Seared Salmon with Ginger and Coriander (see page 123) and the Seared Harissa Tuna Steak (see page 116), will also provide you and your guests with omega 3 essential fats to help brain and heart function, skin condition and hormone balance. The beauty of fish is also the speed at which it cooks. This saves you time in the kitchen and dishes like the Thai Fish Cakes (see below and page 124) can even be prepared well in advance, allowing you to relax and enjoy yourself with your friends.

TANDOORI FISH

The herbs and spices used to marinate the fish in this recipe help to tenderise the flesh and add plenty of flavour. They are also long-acknowledged digestion and immune system boosters. Coriander aids digestion, while ginger and garlic are infection-fighters. Turmeric is a powerful anti-inflammatory spice which has been used with great effect to counteract arthritis. I have used cod loin here, but any firm-fleshed white fish would do, such as haddock or pollock. Choosing line-caught fish also helps to avoid the massive depletion of fish stocks caused by deep-sea trawling. Serve this dish with quinoa or brown basmati or low-GL rice, with chopped coriander stirred through for added colour and flavour. The Baked Bhajis (see page 143) and Indian Spiced Butternut Squash (see page 141) would be good accompaniments, too.

Serves 4

2 tsp garam masala

1 tsp ground cumin

1 tsp ground coriander

1 tsp ground turmeric

1 tsp finely ground sea salt

1 tsp grated fresh root ginger

1 garlic clove, crushed

2 tbsp finely chopped fresh coriander

juice of half a lemon

6 tbsp natural yoghurt

4 x 150g (just over 5oz) line-caught cod loin
    fillets, boned and skinned

freshly ground black pepper

1 Make the marinade by mixing all the ingredients except the fish and pepper together in a large bowl.

2 Coat the fish completely in the marinade, cover and put in the fridge for 30–60 minutes. Be careful not to leave the fish in the marinade for too long, though, as the lemon juice may turn it mushy.

3 Preheat the grill to medium-hot, then grill the fish for around 15 minutes, turning halfway through, or until the flesh flakes easily when pressed. Sprinkle with black pepper and serve immediately, taking care not to break the fillets when you transfer the fish to the plates.

Cook's Notes
Gluten-free, wheat-free

SEARED HARISSA TUNA STEAK

Tuna is often a great favourite with people who love meat, but who are trying to reduce their intake, or those who aren't usually fans of fish, as it doesn't taste particularly 'fishy'. In this recipe, that meaty flavour and firm texture take the strong spices of the hot North African harissa paste well.

When you buy the tuna, choose bright, red-coloured, rather than dull, grey, steaks to ensure maximum freshness. Fresh tuna, which contains beneficial omega 3 essential fat (although in smaller amounts than salmon), can be eaten raw, so serve it as rare or as well done as you like. Some people like to see a 'sandwich' effect, with the outside seared and the middle still bright red. Unfortunately, however, carnivorous fish such as tuna, marlin and swordfish shouldn't be eaten more than once a month due to their heavy metal contamination from the polluted oceans. Serve with a mixed salad and Roast New Potatoes (see page 139).

Serves 4

4 tbsp harissa

2 tbsp lemon juice

4 tuna steaks, washed and patted dry

2 tsp coconut oil or medium or mild (not extra virgin) olive oil

1 Mix the harissa with the lemon juice and spread over the tuna to coat thoroughly on all sides. Put the fish in the fridge to marinate for, ideally, 2 hours, but if you only 10 minutes that will still make a difference and don't worry if you have no time at all.

2 Heat the oil in a large frying pan and add the tuna steaks. Cook on a fairly high heat for 2–3 minutes, at which point, if you look at the side of the steaks, you will see the flesh at the base turning grey as it cooks. Then turn and repeat on the other side.

Cook's Notes

Gluten-free, wheat-free, dairy-free, yeast-free

SMOKED HADDOCK WITH LEEK AND PARSLEY SAUCE

In this recipe tahini – ground sesame paste – is used instead of a standard white sauce as it is dairy-free and rich in minerals and protein. It combines with water and a little bouillon to produce a rich, creamy sauce that is the perfect foil for the smoky, salty fish. Buy undyed haddock fillets if at all possible, to avoid artificial colourings, but if you can't get hold of smoked haddock, use hot-smoked trout instead. The trout won't need cooking, but should be warmed through gently. Serve with the Roast New Potatoes (see page 139).

Serves 4

2 tsp coconut oil or mild or medium (not extra virgin) olive oil

4 large leeks, rinsed and finely sliced

4 tbsp tahini

2 heaped tsp vegetable bouillon powder

4 tbsp flat leaf parsley, finely chopped

4 x 125g (4½oz) undyed smoked haddock loin fillets

1 Heat the oil in a large saucepan and add the leeks. Sauté them for a couple of minutes, then cover them and sweat them for 5–10 minutes, until they soften.

2 Meanwhile, stir together the tahini, bouillon powder and 8 tablespoons of water. Don't worry if it curdles, as stirring will bring it back together.

3 Pour the tahini liquid over the leeks and stir until the sauce has a thick, creamy consistency. Stir in the parsley, taste and check the seasoning. You can always add a little more bouillon powder or water if you need to.

4 Place the fish in a large shallow pan of barely simmering water, making sure that the fillets are covered, and poach gently for 4–5 minutes or until the flesh flakes easily when pressed. Remove the fish from the pan and drain on kitchen paper.

5 Plate up the fish and sauce, sprinkle with black pepper and serve with potatoes.

Cook's Notes
Gluten-free, wheat-free, dairy-free

NASI GORENG

This classic Indonesian street food, which translates simply as 'fried rice', is endlessly varied and variable, and consists of rice fried in a wok with any meat, fish, eggs and vegetables. Vegetarians could easily substitute toasted cashew nuts for the prawns in this version. I recommend using brown basmati or low-GL rice instead of refined white rice to make this much lower GL so that it is filling, not fattening. Get everything ready before you start cooking this dish as it's fast and furious.

Serves 4

300g (10^1/$_2$oz) brown basmati or low-GL rice

1 tbsp coconut oil or mild or medium (not extra virgin) olive oil for cooking the prawns, plus 3 tbsp

1 tsp sambel tomat (Indonesian chilli sauce) or chilli sauce for cooking the prawns, plus 2 tbsp for serving

450g (1lb) raw, shelled fresh prawns

6 shallots, finely sliced

4 garlic cloves, crushed

^{1}/$_2$ a Chinese leaf or white cabbage, shredded

400g (14oz) beansprouts

100g (4oz) frozen peas

2 tbsp nam pla or Thai fish sauce

4 free-range or organic eggs, beaten

juice of 1 lime

1 Cook the rice following the instructions on the packet but do not add salt or stock or it will be too salty once the fish sauce is added. Drain if necessary and cool.

2 Heat a tablespoon of the oil in a wok or frying pan and add a teaspoon or so of the chilli sauce. Stir-fry the prawns for 3 minutes until they sear and turn pink. Remove from the pan and reserve.

3 Add the remaining oil to the pan and stir-fry the shallots and garlic on a very hot heat for 1 minute. Add the Chinese leaf, beansprouts and peas, and stir-fry for another minute. Add the rest of the chilli sauce and stir in.

4 Pour in the eggs and stir-fry for 30 seconds before adding the cooked rice. Stir for a minute or so, then season with the fish sauce, add the reserved prawns and stir it all together.

5 Squeeze fresh lime juice over the top and serve immediately, with extra sambel tomat for those who want it.

Cook's Notes
Gluten-free, wheat-free, dairy-free

SEA BREAM EN PAPILLOTTE

This whole recipe can be prepared, cooked and served in just 30 minutes. Cooking en papillotte (in a parcel of baking paper) allows the fish to steam inside and retain all its moisture and nutrients. This light, zesty dish is incredibly low in fat and is packed with health-boosting herbs and spices to aid digestion. My husband Nick likes it served with quinoa, with plenty of finely chopped coriander and spinach, a drizzle of toasted sesame oil and lime or lemon juice stirred through it, but you could also serve it with brown basmati or low-GL rice and Soy and Sesame Steam-fried Tenderstem (see page 150).

Serves 4

2 x 400g (14oz) whole sea bream, scaled and
   gutted

1 mild red chilli, deseeded and finely sliced

1 tsp grated root ginger

6 spring onions, finely sliced on the diagonal

zest and juice of 1 lime

4 tbsp soy sauce or tamari

2 tbsp rice vinegar

1 tbsp chopped coriander

1 Preheat the oven to 200°C/400°F/gas mark 6. Cut out a large piece of baking paper, big enough to enclose both fish, and place it on a baking tray. Brush the paper lightly with oil before placing the fish side by side in the middle.

2 Mix the chilli, ginger, spring onions and lime zest together. Stuff each fish with a little of this mixture, but spread most of it on top. Spoon the soy or tamari and rice vinegar over the fish and fold up the parcel of baking paper to enclose them.

3 Pop the baking tray into the oven for 20 minutes. Check to see that the fish is cooked – the flesh should flake easily when pressed – and re-fold the parcel and cook for a further few minutes if necessary.

4 When ready, open the parcel, drizzle the fish with a good squeeze of lime juice and scatter with coriander. Carefully transfer the fish to a large platter, so that you can fillet fish straight onto people's plates at the table, spooning the delicious cooking liquor over the top.

Cook's Notes
Gluten-free, wheat-free if you use tamari, dairy-free

SEA BASS WITH BRAISED FENNEL AND ROAST NEW POTATOES

Fish and fennel are a flavour marriage made in heaven and a common combination on French menus. Sea bass is very low in fat, but if you can't get it, you can use any kind of fish – trout would work well. Fennel is considered to be very beneficial to the liver, aiding detoxification. This is a very easy recipe to make and is light enough (if you hold back on the potatoes) to make a delicious summer's lunch or to balance a particularly decadent pudding.

Serves 4

4 servings of Braised Fennel (see page 149)
4 servings Roast New Potatoes (see page 139)
4 x 125g (4¹/₂oz) sea bass fillets

1 tbsp mild or medium (not extra virgin) olive oil
1 lemon, sliced into wedges
freshly ground black pepper

1 Preheat the oven to 180°C/350°F/gas mark 4.

2 Meanwhile, make the Braised Fennel then, when the oven is up to temperature, cook the Roast New Potatoes for around an hour.

3 Wash the fish, pat it dry and season it with a little salt.

4 When the potatoes are ready, heat the oil in a large frying pan and fry the fish for 4–6 minutes, turning halfway through when the bottom is starting to look white and cooked, to make the skin crisp. Don't get distracted at this stage as over-cooking the fish will ruin the delicate texture and flavour.

5 Serve immediately, accompanied by the potatoes, fennel, a little of the fennel's braising liquor if there is any left over, some lemon wedges to squeeze over the top and lots of freshly ground black pepper.

Cook's Notes
Gluten-free, wheat-free, dairy-free, yeast-free

SEARED SALMON WITH GINGER AND CORIANDER

This Thai-inspired dish is packed with Oriental flavours and the large amount of ginger will give your immune system – not to mention your libido – a real boost, thanks to the high zinc content. The refreshing coriander serves to balance the zesty flavour of the ginger and lime, as well as acting as a digestive aid. Salmon is also, of course, rich in omega 3 essential fats to help brain, heart and skin health. Serve with brown basmati or low-GL rice, or soba noodles, and stir-fried vegetables – try the Soy and Sesame Steam-fried Tenderstem (see page 150).

Serves 4

4 x 100g (4oz) salmon fillets, skin on

a little olive oil and salt for rubbing

1 tbsp coconut oil or mild or medium (not extra virgin) olive oil

2 tbsp root ginger, peeled

10 spring onions, topped, tailed and halved

1 tbsp fresh coriander

3 tbsp tamari or soy sauce

3 tbsp toasted sesame oil

juice of 2 limes or lemons

1 Rub the salmon fillets all over with the olive oil and sea salt, and set them aside.

2 Whiz the ginger, spring onions, coriander, tamari or soy, sesame oil, lime juice and 3 tablespoons of water together in a blender until they form a relatively smooth sauce and the ginger is finely chopped. Taste and adjust the seasoning according to taste.

3 Heat the oil in a large frying pan, then pan-fry the salmon fillets for 5–7 minutes on each side or until cooked and the flesh flakes easily when pressed. Serve immediately with the sauce.

Cook's Notes

Wheat-free if you use tamari, dairy-free

THAI FISH CAKES

These are quite, quite delicious and another of my husband Nick's great favourites. Needless to say, though, they are light years away from the type of fish cakes that are stuffed to the gills with potato, milk and butter. This is a light, highly flavoured, Oriental-style cake packed with nutritious superfoods. Serve with rice and steam-fried or stir-fried vegetables and the dipping sauce.

Serves 4

For the cakes

4 garlic cloves, crushed

2 large mild, red chillies, deseeded

2 tbsp root ginger, peeled

4 spring onions, topped and tailed

grated zest of 2 limes

4 tbsp coriander

4 tbsp tamari, soy sauce or fish sauce

2 tbsp toasted sesame oil

4 x 125g (4¹/₂oz) salmon, haddock, cod or hake fillets, skinned and boned

4 tbsp cornflour

1 tbsp coconut oil or mild or medium (not extra virgin) olive oil

For the sauce

2 tbsp toasted sesame oil

2 tbsp tamari or soy sauce

juice of 2 limes

8 spring onions, finely chopped

4 tbsp coriander, finely chopped

2 tbsp sesame seeds, lightly toasted in a dry frying pan

1 Put the garlic, chilli, ginger, spring onions, lime zest and coriander into a food processor with the tamari, soy or fish sauce and sesame oil and blend. Add the fish and blend until the mixture is finely chopped but not entirely smooth.

2 Shape the mixture into 12 patties, squash them down into flat circles and dust them lightly with flour. Place them in the fridge to firm up.

3 To make the dipping sauce, blend the sesame oil, tamari or soy, lime juice, spring onions and coriander together until smooth, then stir in the sesame seeds.

4 Heat the oil in a large frying pan or wok and fry the fish cakes for 3–4 minutes on each side until golden. You will need to do this in batches. Drain on kitchen paper and serve with the dipping sauce.

Cook's Notes

Wheat-free if you use tamari, dairy-free

VEGETARIAN MAIN COURSES

THESE DISHES ARE, I hope, music to the ears of vegetarians sick of the usual suspects offered by unimaginative hosts or restaurants. The fail-safe vegetarian staple is, of course, cheese, but there are many other ways of meeting protein requirements, as showcased here. I use a combination of whole grains and pulses, which top up any amino acid shortfall in each other, to create perfect protein, as in the Chickpea and Cauliflower Curry served with brown rice (see page 135). I also use quinoa, which contains complete protein and which makes an interesting and more nutritious alternative to couscous or bulgar wheat – try the Quinoa with Sun-blush Tomatoes and Olives (see page 131). Nuts and seeds, as in the Sesame Soba Noodle Salad (see opposite) also feature strongly. All these imaginative, balanced dishes show you that there is much more to offer vegetarians than pasta with a cheese sauce.

So why is it so important to include protein in a meal? 'Complete protein' means that a food or meal provides all the eight amino acids which are essential to health and which must be obtained from our diet. Animal foods such as meat, fish, eggs and dairy products provide these amino acids naturally, but plant-based foods need a little more consideration. Nuts, seeds, quinoa, and soya are also good sources of protein, but beans and pulses, such as lentils, chickpeas and kidney beans fall short, as do grains. By combining the two, however, you can top up any shortfalls to create complete protein. This approach is known as 'protein complementarity'.

Sufficient protein allows your body to grow, which is particularly important for children, of course; to repair and rebuild; to keep blood sugar balanced for stable weight and energy levels, because protein is digested more slowly than carbohydrates, slowing down the rate of sugar release from a meal; to build neurotransmitters that allow your brain to process information; and, lastly, to facilitate detoxification of waste products and toxins such as alcohol by the liver.

SESAME SOBA NOODLE SALAD

Soba noodles are made from buckwheat, which, despite the name, is gluten free. This dish is best eaten Japanese-style, in bowls with much slurping, and it's definitely not one to cook for a first dinner date when you want to impress, as noodle dishes are somewhat taxing on one's table manners. The ginger gives this dish a powerful anti-inflammatory punch to help fight infection. It's also rich in zinc to boost the libido and give you glowing skin. You could accompany this with the Soy and Sesame Steam-fried Tenderstem (see page 150) or any other stir-fried vegetables.

Serves 4

400g (14oz) soba noodles

4 heaped tbsp peeled and roughly chopped root ginger

4 tbsp toasted sesame oil

4 tbsp freshly squeezed lime or lemon juice

4 tbsp tamari or soy sauce

400g (14oz) ready-to-eat smoked tofu, cubed

1/2 large cucumber, very finely sliced

4 tbsp sesame seeds, lightly toasted in a dry frying pan until they start to turn golden

1 Cook the noodles according to the pack instructions. Soba noodles usually require boiling for 5 minutes then refreshing in cold water.

2 To make the dressing, in a blender, whiz together the ginger, sesame oil, lime or lemon juice and tamari or soy until smooth – or as smooth as you can get the ginger in your blender. Some bits will probably remain, which is fine.

3 Pour the dressing over the noodles, add the tofu cubes and cucumber slices, and toss together. Heap into bowls and scatter with the toasted sesame seeds.

Cook's Notes

Gluten-free, wheat-free if you use tamari, dairy-free • V • Can be made in advance

GRIDDLED HALLOUMI ON HERBED COUSCOUS

Inspired by Middle Eastern taboulleh, this vibrantly-coloured dish gets colour and flavour from the aromatic herbs. It doesn't need added salt as the halloumi cheese is very salty. Enjoy it on its own, with a mixed leaf salad or with Marinated Griddled Courgettes (see page 145). If you are avoiding wheat, then use barley couscous (you'll find it in good supermarkets) or quinoa.

Serves 4

300g (10^1/2oz) couscous

1 heaped tbsp finely chopped coriander

1 heaped tbsp finely chopped flat-leaf parsley

1 heaped tbsp finely chopped mint

juice of 1^1/2 lemons

2 red peppers, sliced into long, thick strips

1 tbsp medium or mild (not extra virgin) olive oil

500g (1lb 2oz) halloumi, cut into 12 slices

2 avocados

freshly ground black pepper

1 Cook the couscous according to the pack instructions. Set to one side to cool and, when it's fairly cool, stir in the herbs and the juice from one lemon.

2 Heat a griddle pan until it's smoking. Place the pepper slices in a bowl and pour the oil over them, stirring to coat them. Griddle them for 15 minutes, turning them once, until they are soft. Set to one side.

3 Griddle the halloumi slices until the bottom comes away from the pan without sticking (this can take up to 5 minutes). Then turn them. Do the same for the other side. Repeat until all the slices are done.

4 Place a mound of couscous on each plate and arrange pepper slices over each pile.

5 Slice the avocados in half, extract the stone, then slice the flesh lengthways and scoop it out with a spoon.

6 Lay the avocado slices on the couscous mounds and top with the halloumi.

7 Sprinkle the remaining lemon juice over each plate to prevent the avocados going brown. Top with freshly ground black pepper.

Cook's Notes

V • Can be made in advance, but don't add the herbs to the couscous or cook the halloumi until you're ready to serve

BAKED FALAFEL

The exact origins of this popular dish are controversial – the Indians claim it as their own although it is commonly thought to be a Middle Eastern dish. Either way, these baked chickpea balls are delicious with a dollop of Hummus (see page 87) and a red onion, tomato and coriander salad, stuffed in a toasted wholemeal pitta bread or served with quinoa or couscous, with a large wedge of lemon per person to squeeze over the top and bring out the flavour. I oven-bake my version to limit the oil and trans fats found in deep-fried, shop-bought versions, but there is no loss of flavour.

Serves 4

2 x 410g cans chickpeas, rinsed and drained, or
   275g (10oz) dried chickpeas, cooked
4 garlic cloves, crushed
4 tsp tahini
10 spring onions, roughly sliced
50g (2oz) sesame seeds

4 tsp ground cumin
2 tsp ground coriander
2 tbsp flat leaf parsley, finely chopped
2 tsp sea salt and freshly ground black pepper
2 medium organic or free-range eggs
60g (2¹/₂oz) sesame seeds for coating

1 Preheat the oven to 200°C/400°F/gas mark 6. Line a baking tray with non-stick baking paper.

2 Place all the ingredients bar the salt, pepper, egg and sesame seeds in a food processor and blend until fairly smooth and combined. Taste and season accordingly. Mix in the beaten egg and shape into 16 golf ball-sized balls.

3 Put the sesame seeds on a plate and roll the balls in them. This is a bit fiddly, so you may prefer to scatter the seeds over each side of the falafel. It might be necessary to then reshape the falafel in your hand.

4 Place the balls on the baking tray and cook for 20–25 minutes or until just golden on top and firm to the touch.

Cook's Notes
Gluten-free, wheat-free, dairy-free, yeast-free • V • Can be made in advance • Suitable for freezing

QUINOA WITH SUN-BLUSH TOMATOES AND OLIVES

This delicious, easy mixture is ideal for anyone with food sensitivities, as it is gluten-, wheat- and dairy-free. It also has no added salt, other than that in the olives, but doesn't taste bland thanks to the full-flavoured Mediterranean ingredients. The plentiful herbs, leaves and garlic make it a great source of antioxidants to protect your skin and health, while the quinoa contains all the eight essential amino acids that make up complete protein, as well as providing more calcium than milk. A simple, light recipe for an informal meal or to serve at a barbecue, this dish would go well with a mixed salad and avocado slices.

Serves 4

300g (10^1/$_2$oz) quinoa

1 tbsp coconut oil or medium or mild (not extra virgin) olive oil

1 red onion, diced

2 courgettes, diced

juice of 1 lemon

2 handfuls of basil leaves

2 handfuls of flat leaf parsley

2 handfuls of rocket and/or watercress

2 handfuls of baby leaf spinach

1 garlic clove, crushed

freshly ground black pepper

175g (6oz) pitted Kalamata olives

175g (6oz) sun-blush tomatoes

1 Place the quinoa in a large saucepan, add double the amount of water and bring to the boil. Cover and simmer for 10 minutes then rest, covered, for 5 minutes to allow the grains to become soft and fluffy.

2 Meanwhile, heat the oil in a large frying pan and sauté the onion and courgette for a minute. Then cover and sweat for around 5 minutes to soften them.

3 Place the lemon juice, herbs and leaves, garlic and black pepper in a blender or food processer and blitz until the leaves are finely chopped. Add the olives and sun-blush tomatoes and blend briefly until they are coarsely chopped and combined.

4 Stir the cooked vegetables and the olive mixture into the quinoa and taste to check the seasoning. Serve warm or cold.

Cook's Notes

Gluten-free, wheat-free, dairy-free • V • Can be made in advance

MUSHROOM AND POT BARLEY RISOTTO

Barley is a traditional ingredient in Scottish cooking, where it appears in hearty, warming broths and stews. Here it's used in the Italian equivalent – a risotto. In fact, it makes a much easier risotto than rice, as barley doesn't need nearly so much attention during cooking – just pour on the stock and leave it to simmer. Pot barley (unlike pearl barley) is the whole grain and is a good source of protein, fibre and niacin (vitamin B_3), as well as the trace minerals calcium, magnesium, phosphorus and potassium. It needs to be soaked for at least six hours, as this makes it more digestible and reduces the cooking time. I sometimes serve this with the Marinated Griddled Courgettes (see page 145) to further the Italian theme.

Serves 4

2 tbsp coconut oil or mild or medium (not
  extra virgin) olive oil or butter
2 white onions, finely chopped
300g (10½oz) assorted fresh mushrooms, sliced
300g (10½oz) pot barley, soaked overnight
  and drained
25g (1oz) dried porcini mushrooms, soaked for
  30 minutes and drained (add the soaking
  liquor to the stock)

1.2L (2pt) hot vegetable stock, including the
  soaking liquor from the dried mushrooms
freshly ground black pepper
a little sea salt to taste
50g (2oz) grated Parmesan
2 tbsp flat leaf parsley, finely chopped

1 Heat the oil or butter in a heavy-based saucepan and gently sweat the onions for 3–4 minutes to soften them. Add the fresh mushrooms and sweat for another 6–8 minutes until they soften as well.

2 Pour in the pot barley and stir frequently for a couple of minutes to toast the grains.

3 Add the dried mushrooms and stir for a few minutes. Now add the hot stock and let the barley simmer, stirring occasionally, until it has absorbed all the liquid. This should take around an hour.

4 Season to taste with black pepper and a little salt, then dollop onto plates, and scatter with the Parmesan and parsley.

Cook's Notes
Wheat-free if you use a wheat-free stock, dairy-free if you omit the Parmesan, yeast-free • V • Can be made in advance, but warm the risotto through and add the parsley when you're ready to serve

LENTIL AND SQUASH CURRY

This curry is very easy to make and is bursting with flavour from the spices, garlic, onion and spinach. It's an ideal dish to serve in the winter when we could all benefit from topping up our infection-busting antioxidant reserves via the garlic and onion. In fact, this dish is jam-packed with fibre to aid digestion, and vitamins and phytonutrients (plant nutrients) to help us to stave off illness. Serve with brown basmati or low-GL rice for a protein-packed vegetarian main meal.

Serves 4

1 tbsp mild or medium (not extra virgin) olive oil

2 red onions, chopped

4 garlic cloves, crushed

1 medium butternut squash, unpeeled, deseeded and cubed

2 tbsp curry powder

600ml (1pt) vegetable stock

100g (4oz) dried split red lentils, rinsed and drained

400g can tomatoes, chopped

4 tbsp baby leaf spinach

2 tsp sea salt

freshly ground black pepper

handful of coriander, finely chopped

1 Heat the oil in a saucepan and gently sweat the onion and garlic for around 5 minutes to soften them.

2 Stir in the butternut squash and curry powder, then pour in the stock, lentils and tomatoes, and bring to the boil. Cover and simmer for around an hour, stirring occasionally, to let the squash soften and the sauce reduce.

3 Stir in the spinach, cover for a few minutes while it wilts, then season to taste with the salt, pepper and coriander.

Cook's Notes
Gluten-free, wheat-free if you use a wheat-free stock, dairy-free • V • Can be made in advance • Suitable for freezing, but don't add the spinach until you've defrosted and reheated the curry

CHICKPEA AND CAULIFLOWER CURRY

India has some of the finest vegetarian dishes in the world, packed with flavour, thanks to the liberal use of herbs and spices combined with vegetables. The turmeric in the curry paste gives this curry anti-inflammatory properties to offer relief from allergy symptoms, joint pains and skin problems. When you buy the coconut milk, don't get a reduced-fat version as many of coconut's renowned health properties are found in the fat. This curry is also very quick to make and can be served with brown basmati or low-GL rice, or quinoa.

Serves 4

2 tbsp coconut oil or mild or medium (not extra virgin) olive oil

3 tbsp medium curry paste

2 large onions, sliced

1/2 cauliflower, broken into small florets

410g can chickpeas, rinsed and drained

400ml can coconut milk

210ml (7fl oz) hot vegetable stock

1 tbsp tamari or soy sauce

250g (9oz) fine green beans

handful of coriander, torn or roughly chopped

a little sea salt

1 Put the oil and the curry paste in a large frying pan or wok and fry the onions over a medium heat for around 5 minutes to soften them. Add the cauliflower and chickpeas to the pan and stir to coat them in the other ingredients.

2 Pour in the coconut milk, stock and tamari, and stir. Bring to the boil, then cover and simmer over a gentle heat for around 30 minutes or until the cauliflower is fairly soft.

3 Stir in the green beans and cook for another 5 minutes or so until they're tender. Check the seasoning, add salt if necessary and scatter with the coriander leaves before serving.

Cook's Notes

Gluten-free, wheat-free if you use tamari, dairy-free • V • Can be made in advance, but add the green beans and warm the curry through when you're ready to serve

WILD RICE AND PUY LENTILS WITH LEMON AND ASPARAGUS

This dish is bursting with refreshing summer flavours, such as citrus and asparagus, and makes an ideal summer lunch or supper as it can be prepared in advance. Wild rice is not, in fact, a rice at all, but a grass that is particularly rich in protein and minerals. Accompany this dish with a red onion, tomato, avocado and basil salad.

Serves 6

250g (9oz) wild rice
150g (5¹/₂oz) dried Puy lentils
1 tsp vegetable bouillon powder
2 courgettes
8 spring onions, trimmed
200g (7oz) fine asparagus spears

4 tbsp mild or medium (not extra virgin) olive oil
juice of 2 lemons plus zest and juice of 2 more organic or unwaxed lemons
4 tbsp extra virgin olive oil
freshly ground black pepper
a little sea salt

1 Place the rice and lentils in a large saucepan and cover with boiling water. Soak for 4 hours to soften and reduce the cooking time, then drain, return to the saucepan with the vegetable bouillon and re-cover with 600ml (1pt) of boiling water. Bring to the boil then cover and simmer for 20 minutes or until cooked and the water has been absorbed.

2 Meanwhile, top and tail the courgettes and slice them very finely using a mandolin. Place in a large bowl with the spring onions and asparagus, and pour the lemon juice and mild or medium olive oil over them, stirring to coat, then leave to marinate for at least 10 minutes.

3 Preheat a griddle pan until smoking then griddle the courgette strips very quickly in batches, turning to colour on both sides. Add to the cooked rice and lentils. Then griddle the spring onions for around 4–5 minutes, rolling occasionally to colour evenly, then add to the rice and lentils. Next griddle the asparagus – in batches if necessary – for around 5 minutes, rolling occasionally to cook evenly. Pour a few tablespoons of the leftover marinade into the griddle pan to par-steam the asparagus for a minute or two until soft. Add the asparagus to the rice and lentils.

4 Fold the griddled vegetables into the rice and lentils, along with the zest and juice of the remaining two lemons, the extra virgin olive oil, black pepper and salt to taste. Serve warm or at room temperature.

Cook's Notes
Gluten-free, wheat-free, dairy-free, yeast-free • V • Can be made in advance

ACCOMPANIMENTS

SIDE DISHES ARE a good way to increase the vegetable and whole grain content of a meal to boost fibre intake and therefore aid digestion. Adequate fibre is particularly important to aid digestion when we eat a meal rich in animal protein and animal fat, so if you're serving a meat- or cheese-based main course, make sure that you partner it with plenty of fresh vegetables and whole grains to help the body process the food quickly and comfortably.

You will see that the recipes here make full use of a range of colourful, flavoursome vegetables, pulses and whole grains – from the Marinated Griddled Courgettes (see page 145), which is the perfect partner to Mediterranean dishes, to the Oriental-inspired Soy and Sesame Steam-fried Tenderstem (see page 150) and the Indian Spiced Butternut Squash (see page 141). By eating a range of different coloured fruits and vegetables you ensure that you consume a full spectrum of phytonutrients (plant nutrients), which have all manner of miraculous health properties, from the skin- and eye-enhancing betacarotene in orange coloured foods like squash, sweet potatoes and mango, to the sulforaphane and the indoles in dark green cruciferous vegetables like broccoli, which have been shown to exhibit anti-cancer effects.

ROAST NEW POTATOES

This is the easiest way to roast potatoes, with no skinning or basting required. The skins become deliciously crisp and retain extra goodness, and the recipe uses far less fat than the traditional method. Plus, by using baby new potatoes, you avoid the high starch content of larger, older potatoes, keeping the GL of the dish low. Serve with roast dishes like the Rosemary and Garlic Roast Lamb (see page 103) or the Sea Bass with Braised Fennel (see page 121).

Serves 4

700g (just over 1^1/$_2$lb) baby new potatoes

drizzle of mild or medium (not extra virgin) olive oil

sprinkle of sea salt

1 Preheat the oven to 180°C/350°F/gas mark 4.

2 Rinse and dry the new potatoes and chop any large ones in half, so they are all roughly the same size and will cook evenly. Place the potatoes in a roasting tin and drizzle with a little oil then sprinkle with sea salt. Shake the tin to coat the potatoes evenly and place in the oven.

3 Cook the potatoes for about an hour, taking the tray out and shaking halfway through to turn the potatoes.

Cook's Notes

Gluten-free, wheat-free, dairy-free • V

CASHEW AND HERB CORN BREAD

Corn bread is a good gluten-free alternative to wheat bread, which can be hard to digest and is linked to IBS. This loaf also benefits from being made with half corn meal and half ground cashew nuts. The nuts increase the protein content and help to keep the GL of the bread low, to leave you fuller for longer. This bread is delicious served with Hummus (see page 87), or Guacamole (see page 89), the Vegetable Antipasti Mezze (see page 89) or a leaf salad. If you have any leftovers, they can be frozen.

Serves 12

150g (5¹/₂oz) fine corn meal or polenta

150g (5¹/₂oz) unroasted, unsalted cashew nuts, ground

1 tbsp Mediterranean mixed dried herbs or Italian seasoning

1 tsp sea salt

4 tsp baking powder (gluten-free if necessary)

225ml (around 7¹/₂fl oz) milk or unsweetened non-dairy milk such as oat or rice milk

3 medium free-range or organic eggs

5 tbsp mild or medium (not extra virgin) olive oil

1 Preheat the oven to 200°C/400°F/gas mark 6. Line a baking tray of about 20cm x 30cm (8in x 12in) in size with baking paper.

2 Place the corn meal, ground cashews, herbs and salt in a mixing bowl and sieve the baking powder on top. Stir to mix thoroughly.

3 Stir the milk, eggs and oil together in a bowl or jug and pour into the dry ingredients, stirring to form a loose dough.

4 Pour onto the prepared baking tray and bake for 25 minutes, until golden on top and firm to the touch. Cool on a wire rack then cut into squares and store in an airtight container.

Cook's Notes

Gluten-free, wheat-free, dairy-free if you use non-dairy milk, yeast-free • V • Can be made in advance • Suitable for freezing

INDIAN SPICED BUTTERNUT SQUASH

The bright orange flesh of squashes shows their high beta-carotene content. This antioxidant pro-vitamin is important for eye and skin health, as it's converted in the body into vitamin A. Squash makes an interesting change from the standard carbohydrate accompaniments of pasta, rice or potatoes, as well as providing plenty of fibre, vitamins and slow-releasing, low-GL energy. The mild spices add flavour without the need for extra salt. Serve this as a side dish with curries or with the Tandoori Fish (see page 115) instead of, or in addition to, rice.

Serves 4

950g (2lb 2oz) butternut squash, washed but unpeeled
1/2 tsp turmeric
1 1/2 tsp ground cumin

1 1/2 tsp ground coriander
1 tsp of sea salt
2 tbsp tomato purée
1 tbsp mild or medium (not extra virgin) olive oil

1 Preheat the oven to 200°C/400°F/gas mark 6.

2 Cut the butternut squash in half lengthways and scrape out the seeds and pulp with a spoon. Cut each half into four, lengthways, so you have eight long pieces in total.

3 Mix the turmeric, cumin, coriander, salt, tomato purée and oil together in a bowl, then rub the paste all over the squash until evenly coated.

4 Place the squash in a roasting dish and cook for 45–60 minutes or until the flesh is soft when pierced or squashed, removing from the oven halfway through to turn the pieces over.

Cook's Notes
Gluten-free, wheat-free, dairy-free, yeast-free • V • Can be made in advance

BAKED BHAJIS

This is a healthier, baked version of the Indian classic, so my recipe uses fibre and protein-rich chickpeas rather than stodgy potato, plus spinach for beta-carotene and iron. These bhajis are also baked rather than deep-fried, to cut down on the fat content. They are delicious served with a curry, such as the Lentil and Squash Curry (see page 134) or the Chickpea and Cauliflower Curry (see page 135), and a little brown basmati or low-GL rice, or the Tandoori Fish (see page 115). Serve with a large wedge of lemon or lime per person to squeeze over the bhajis and bring out the flavour.

Serves 4

1 tbsp mild or medium (not extra virgin) olive oil

2 red onions, diced

2 garlic cloves, crushed

4 tsp curry powder

150g (5^1/$_2$oz) baby leaf spinach

2 x 410g cans chickpeas, rinsed and drained, or 275g (9^3/$_4$oz) dried chickpeas, cooked

2 heaped tbsp finely chopped coriander

2 tsp sea salt

2 medium free-range or organic eggs, beaten

1 Preheat the oven to 180°C/350°F/gas mark 4. Line a baking tray with non-stick baking paper.

2 Heat the oil in a small pan and sweat the onion and garlic with the curry powder for around 5 minutes to soften. Add the spinach to the pan and stir to wilt for a further minute or so.

3 Place all the other ingredients bar the eggs in a food processor and blend until fairly smooth and combined. Mix in the beaten egg, shape into 16 patties and place on the baking tray.

4 Cook the bhajis for around 25 minutes or until firm to the touch.

Cook's Notes

Gluten-free, wheat-free, dairy-free, yeast-free • V • Can be made in advance • Suitable for freezing

ROASTED MEDITERRANEAN VEGETABLES

This is a full-flavoured way to up your intake of vegetables and benefit from their fibre, vitamins and antioxidants. You can vary the vegetables according to your likes or dislikes and which ones are in season. Do use the rosemary, though. Apart from its wonderful fragrance, rosemary contains substances that improve digestion, increase circulation (including to the brain, helping concentration), stimulate the immune system and reduce inflammation. Plus its high antioxidant content helps to offset any damage to the ingredients by oxidation at high temperatures that may occur during roasting. This dish is a good all-rounder that's excellent with Mediterranean flavours such as the Rosemary and Garlic Roast Lamb (see page 103).

Serves 4

2 courgettes, roughly chopped into bite-sized chunks

2 red onions, roughly chopped into wedges

2 red, yellow or orange peppers, roughly chopped into bite-sized chunks

4 garlic cloves, unpeeled

2 tbsp medium or mild (not extra virgin) olive oil

2 sprigs of rosemary

1 Preheat the oven to 180°C/350°F/gas mark 4.

2 Place the courgettes, onions, peppers and garlic in a roasting tin. I've said to leave the garlic unpeeled, because the skin protects the garlic from burning, ensuring a naturally sweet flavour and maximum nutrients, and the softened cloves squeeze out of their skins easily after cooking. Drizzle with the oil, stir to coat evenly, then put the rosemary on top.

3 Place the tray in the oven for around 45 minutes to an hour, taking it out and stirring halfway through to turn the vegetables.

4 When the vegetables are cooked – they should be soft when pierced – remove the rosemary stalks, discard them and serve.

Cook's Notes
Gluten-free, wheat-free, dairy-free, yeast-free • V • Can be made in advance

MARINATED GRIDDLED COURGETTES

With chargrilled stripes on the courgettes from the griddle pan, this recipe looks as good as it tastes. However, as the courgettes are not on the griddle for long and are coated in the antioxidant preservative vitamin C, from the lemon juice, there is minimal nutrient loss. If you don't have a griddle you could grill the courgettes at a very high heat for a couple of minutes. This dish is delicious with the Griddled Halloumi on Herbed Couscous (see page 128).

Serves 4

4 medium-sized courgettes
juice of 1 lemon

4 tbsp medium or mild (not extra virgin) olive oil

1 Top and tail the courgettes, then slice them finely lengthways. This is easier and neater when done using a mandolin, rather than a knife, but either works. You should get around 12 strips from each courgette.

2 Place the courgette strips in a large bowl and pour the lemon juice and oil over them. Mix to coat thoroughly and leave to marinate for at least 10 minutes, ideally 20–30 minutes.

3 Preheat a griddle pan until very hot and get a large plate ready for the courgettes once cooked. Using tongs, place strips of courgette on the pan until there is no more space. At this point it will be time to turn over the first strips. If you have cut the courgettes more thickly, then they may need a little longer to sear, but you simply want them to pick up some marks and cook a little. It doesn't take long, so stay at the hob and work fairly quickly. Place the cooked courgettes on the plate and continue griddling the courgettes until they are all done. They are best served warm.

Cook's Notes
Gluten-free, wheat-free, dairy-free • V • Can be made in advance, but allow to come up to room temperature before serving

PEPERONATA

This is absolutely delicious – soft, sweet, slow-roasted peppers, onions and tomatoes with a flavour kick from the olives. Peperonata is the perfect addition to a cold lunch of meats, Cashew and Herb Corn Bread (see page 140) and Hummus (see page 87), or serve warm with the Greek-style Stuffed Pork Tenderloin (see page 108). The bright colours of this dish show how rich it is in carotenoids, which are antioxidants that help to protect your skin and eyes.

Serves 4

5 tbsp medium or mild (not extra virgin) olive oil
6 garlic cloves, sliced
2 red onions, thinly sliced into wedges
2 red peppers, thinly sliced lengthways
2 yellow or orange peppers, thinly sliced
  lengthways

225g (8oz) cherry tomatoes
100g (4oz) Kalamata olives, pitted if you prefer
1 tsp of sea salt
freshly ground black pepper
1 tbsp roughly torn basil

1 Heat the oil in a large pan and gently sweat the garlic and onions for around 10 minutes to soften them.

2 Add the peppers, cover and cook for a further 10 minutes before adding the tomatoes and olives.

3 Simmer for a further 15–20 minutes until the tomatoes soften and burst and all the vegetables are soft. Season with salt and pepper and scatter with the basil leaves. Serve warm or at room temperature.

Cook's Notes
Gluten-free, wheat-free, dairy-free, yeast-free • V • Can be made in advance

WARM FLAGEOLET BEANS WITH HERBS

These delicately flavoured, pale green beans are the perfect partner to lamb and I suggest you serve them with the Rosemary and Garlic Roast Lamb (see page 103). They also make a good low-GL carbohydrate alternative to rice, pasta or potatoes and are rich in fibre and protein.

Serves 4

2 x 410g cans flageolet beans, rinsed
  and drained
1 tbsp extra virgin olive oil
2 tbsp meat or vegetable stock

1 tsp herbes de Provence
juice from roast lamb (if serving with the
  Rosemary and Garlic Roast Lamb)
a little sea salt, to taste (optional)

1 Place the beans in a saucepan with the olive oil, stock and herbs. Simmer very gently for a couple of minutes.

2 If you're serving the beans with Rosemary and Garlic Roast Lamb (see page 103), pour in 2 tablespoons of the juices that have drained from the meat during resting. Simmer to warm through, add salt if required and then serve.

Cook's Notes
Gluten-free, wheat-free if you use a wheat-free stock, dairy-free, yeast-free • V (without meat stock) • Can be made in advance

BRAISED FENNEL

The aniseed flavour of fennel is the perfect partner to fish, so try this with my sea bass recipe (see page 121). Fennel has long been considered a liver tonic which aids detoxification, making this the ideal vegetable choice if you're serving alcohol with your meal.

Serves 4

1 tbsp mild or medium (not extra virgin) olive oil   50ml (2fl oz) vegetable stock
2 fennel bulbs, outer leaves and stalks
    removed, and sliced

1 Heat the oil in a pan and sweat the fennel for around 5–8 minutes, until it starts to soften.

2 Add the stock and braise for around 15 minutes or until very soft and translucent.

Cook's Notes
Gluten-free if you use a gluten-free stock, wheat-free if you use a wheat-free stock, dairy-free
V • Can be made in advance

SOY AND SESAME STEAM-FRIED TENDERSTEM

Tenderstem is the most nutritious type of broccoli and has an incredibly high antioxidant score. To minimise the loss of its valuable nutrients, try to cook it quickly and don't let it go soggy and dull-coloured. Soy and sesame provide a strongly flavoured sauce for any reluctant vegetable-eaters, but if you're short of time cook the tenderstem as instructed and then drizzle it with a little toasted sesame oil and tamari or soy. This dish makes an attractive accompaniment to any Oriental-style dishes, including Nasi Goreng (see page 118) or the Thai Fish Cakes (see page 124).

Serves 4

1 tsp vegetable bouillon powder

1 tsp cornflour

1 tbsp toasted sesame oil

1 tbsp tamari or soy sauce

1 tbsp coconut oil or mild or medium (not extra virgin) olive oil

200g (7oz) tenderstem broccoli

1 Mix all the ingredients except for the tenderstem and coconut or olive oil together in a cup. Add 2 tablespoons of water.

2 Cut the tenderstem spears into three pieces and heat the oil in a wok or large saucepan. Throw in the tenderstem and stir-fry for a couple of minutes, then soak a sheet of kitchen towel in cold water and place this over the tenderstem, to cover the pan. Put the lid on and steam-fry for a couple more minutes, until the vegetables soften a little.

3 Pour in the sauce and allow it to come to the boil, to coat the tenderstem and cook the cornflour.

Cook's Notes

Gluten-free, wheat-free if you use tamari, dairy-free • V • Can be made in advance

SWEET THINGS

WHETHER IT BE a decadent pudding, after-dinner petits fours or a simple slice of cake with afternoon tea – I have to confess that this is my favourite section. In fact, women seem to carry the 'sweet tooth' gene more frequently than men, so if any male readers are cooking with romance in mind, this course above all is going to be the key to a girl's heart. Fortunately, I can help by providing you with a selection of decadent-tasting, but surprisingly virtuous treats to end a meal in style.

If you thought that cakes and puddings were unhealthy, think again. These recipes avoid or dramatically cut down on the usual high-fat dairy products, refined wheat flour and sugar, and get all their delicious flavour from nutritious, natural ingredients, such as fruit and nuts, zesty citrus, warming cinnamon and ginger, and rich dark chocolate. The latter is, you will be thrilled to learn, a health food in its own right!

Good quality dark chocolate is lower in sugar than cheap brands and is packed with magnesium to relax you, iron to oxygenate your cells, the antioxidant procyanidin to help protect your heart, and tryptophan to boost your serotonin levels and put you in a good mood.

If you have used any of the other cookbooks Patrick and I have written, you will be familiar with the sugar alternative xylitol, which we recommend on the Holford Diet and in *Smart Food for Smart Kids*. This naturally occurring sugar alcohol is found in some fruits and vegetables, and has the same sweetness as sugar but doesn't upset blood sugar levels, making it ideal for diabetics and indeed anyone wanting to lose weight or avoid energy slumps. As xylitol is naturally antibacterial, it doesn't rot teeth either, unlike standard sugar. Patrick and I like it not only because it successfully sweetens foods, including baked products, and drinks, but also because it isn't an artificial sweetener stuffed with man-made chemicals that could have unknown side-effects. It is available from most good supermarkets and from health food stores, or online. If you prefer to use ordinary sugar, simply substitute exactly the same amount of sugar for xylitol.

For those of you who, quite rightly, are suspicious of any sugar substitutes, please be reassured by the fact that xylitol is the only sweetener that nutritionists such as Patrick and myself recommend, as research has established its safety. In 1986 the Federation of American Societies for Experimental Biology (FASEB) was commissioned by the US Food and Drug Administration (FDA) to review all relevant data concerning xylitol and other polyols. Their findings indicated xylitol's safety for human consumption and its suitability as an approved food additive for use in foods for special dietary uses.

CHOCOLATE ORANGE MOUSSE

This mousse is simply sublime and you'll find yourself sneaking to the fridge for a spoonful of the leftovers – if there are any! It's the perfect partner for the Strawberry and Banana Cheesecake (see page 154) or serve it with fresh strawberries and/or raspberries. This recipe uses no cream or butter, just simple, unadulterated ingredients which work together perfectly to create the most delicious end to a meal. Ensure you use a chocolate that has 60 per cent cocoa solids, because if it's too dark it will overpower the flavour of the orange. This is best made the day before so it can set overnight, or, at the very latest, make it that morning.

Serves 4

180g (just over 6oz) good quality dark chocolate (60 per cent cocoa solids)

150ml (5fl oz) freshly squeezed or pure (no added sugar) orange juice

6 medium organic or free-range eggs, separated

1 Melt the chocolate over a bain marie or in a microwave. For the bain marie, half fill the saucepan with water and let it simmer. Place the chocolate in a heat-proof bowl and put the bowl over the saucepan, making sure it doesn't touch the water. The chocolate will gently melt over the heat.

2 Add the juice to the bowl and cook with the chocolate over a gentle heat until it forms a creamy consistency. This takes quite a long time and the mixture won't get very thick, but it should be fairly gloopy and move slowly over the back of a spoon.

3 Remove from the heat and beat in the egg yolks, one at a time.

4 Beat the egg whites until they form stiff peaks then gently fold a spoonful of the beaten egg into the chocolate mixture to loosen it, using a metal spoon so as not to knock out all the air. Gently fold in the rest of the egg and carefully spoon the mousse into a large bowl. Immediately place it in the fridge to set.

Cook's Notes

Gluten-free, wheat-free, dairy-free if you use dairy-free chocolate • V • Health note: Because this recipe contains raw egg, always choose organic or at the very least free-range eggs to reduce the likelihood of salmonella contamination, and do not serve to pregnant women, very young children, the elderly or infirm

STRAWBERRY AND BANANA CHEESECAKE

This is an absolutely delicious, yet surprisingly virtuous, cheesecake. If you're serving two puddings and want something to complement it, it's out of this world with the Chocolate Orange Mousse (see page 153). It's wheat-free and packed with minerals, essential fats and protein from the seeds and nuts, as well as being much lower in fat, thanks to the use of yoghurt and cottage cheese in place of traditional cream.

Serves 8–10

For the base

100g (4oz) oat cakes, roughly broken up

100g (4oz) unsalted nuts and/or seeds
   (hazelnuts, almonds, walnuts, Brazil nuts
   and sunflower seeds work well)

50g (2oz) coconut oil or 75g (3oz) butter, melted

30g (just over 1oz) xylitol

1 heaped tbsp ground ginger

For the filling

375g (13oz) plain cottage cheese

300g (10^1/$_2$oz) natural yoghurt

3 tbsp tahini

75g (3oz) xylitol

1 tsp vanilla extract (not artificial vanilla essence)

3 medium ripe bananas

3 good handfuls of strawberries, chopped

1 Preheat the oven to 160°C/325°F/gas mark 3. Line a 20cm (8in) loose-bottomed cake tin with baking paper and grease the sides.

2 Place the oat cakes, nuts, seeds, oil or melted butter, xylitol and ginger in a food processor and whiz until they are the consistency of coarse breadcrumbs. Press firmly into the bottom of the lined cake tin using a metal tablespoon, so that the base is evenly covered. Bake for 10 minutes then turn off the oven and leave the base to cool in the oven with the door ajar.

3 Meanwhile, blend the cottage cheese until really smooth then add the rest of the filling ingredients and blend again until smooth (you want to avoid any little flecks of cottage cheese remaining). Taste and add a little more xylitol to sweeten if necessary. This will very much depend on the sweetness of the bananas and tahini – some brands of tahini are more bitter than others.

4 Pour into the cake tin and cook for around an hour or until the top is just firm to the touch. Allow to cool on a wire rack then scatter the chopped strawberries on top and chill. If you wish, purée some strawberries and drizzle over the top of the cheesecake.

Cook's Notes

Wheat-free • V • Suitable for freezing, but add the strawberries just before serving

CHEESE PLATTER

In order to make this fat-laden course a little healthier, follow my tips for a lighter, more digestible end to the meal. I recommend goat or sheep's milk cheeses, such as feta, soft goat's cheese, Manchego or Pecorino, as these are easier to digest than cow's milk cheeses. Also, go for some soft cheeses as well as hard cheeses, as soft cheese has less saturated fat. I like to go for local cheeses where possible. Lastly, don't just offer biscuits and grapes with the cheese, as fruit and nuts add more flavour, variety and nutrients. I suggest red grapes with their seeds as the seeds contain added nutrients and red grapes are particularly high in the heart-friendly flavonoids quercetin and rutin, which are absent in white grapes.

Serves 4

selection of three cheeses
4 sticks of celery, cut into batons
2 apples, cored and sliced
bunch of red grapes, with seeds

bowl of fresh or dried figs
bowl of fresh, or unsulphured dried, apricots
bowl of walnut halves
12–16 rough oat cakes

Arrange the ingredients on a cheeseboard or large platter and allow people to help themselves. In my experience people pick away at cheeseboards, so although it may seem like quite a lot of celery and fruit, they will help to fill people up without gorging on cheese. They are also a refreshing palate-cleanser after a rich meal.

Cook's Notes
Wheat-free • V • Can be made in advance

COCONUT AND PINEAPPLE SORBET

Sweet, creamy and delicious with fresh fruit such as berries or mango, this is a Caribbean-inspired ice cream-meets-sorbet affair. It can also be served instead of dairy ice cream with the Polenta Citrus Cake (see page 158). Pineapple is the perfect food to end a meal with as it contains bromelain, an enzyme which digests protein, to help you break down your food. Bromelain is also naturally anti-inflammatory, helping to alleviate inflammatory conditions such as asthma, eczema or arthritis.

Serves 6–8

275g (9³/4oz) fresh pineapple
125g (4¹/2oz) xylitol
juice of 1 lime

400ml (just over 13fl oz) canned, full fat coconut milk
100g (4oz) desiccated coconut

1 Blend the pineapple (use canned if you can't get fresh), xylitol and lime juice together until you have a purée. Stir or blend in the coconut milk, then stir in the desiccated coconut.

2 Pour into a freezer-safe container and freeze for an hour, until it's just setting at the edges, then beat well or blend again. Return it to the freezer for at least another 4 hours or overnight, until it's set solid.

3 You can also serve this sorbet while it's still slushy or, if it's frozen solid, remove from the freezer 20–30 minutes before serving to allow it to soften a little, then blend in a food processor to create a thick, creamy consistency and remove any remaining ice crystals (the lack of cream means that it is harder when frozen than dairy ice cream). Alternatively, use an ice cream maker and follow the manufacturer's instructions.

Cook's Notes
Gluten-free, wheat-free, dairy-free, yeast-free • V • Can be made in advance • Suitable for freezing

POLENTA CITRUS CAKE

This recipe is based on one given to me by Liz Lacey, a very dear friend of the McDonald Joyce family. It's a gluten- and dairy-free cake with a beautiful golden colour. Thanks to the corn meal and ground almonds it's dense and moist, and the tart citrus zest and juice stops it from being too sweet. Do try to get unwaxed or organic lemons and oranges, though, to avoid pesticides and wax, and get as much juice and flesh from the fruit as you can. Either serve the cake for tea or as a pudding – it's absolute heaven with the Coconut and Pineapple Sorbet (see page 157).

Serves 10

finely grated zest and juice of 3 lemons

finely grated zest and juice of 2 large oranges

185ml (just over 6fl oz) medium or mild (not extra virgin) olive oil

215g (7½oz) xylitol

3 large free-range or organic eggs

3 drops of almond extract

175g (6oz) fine corn meal/polenta

140g (5oz) ground almonds

1 tsp baking powder (gluten-free if necessary)

75g (3oz) flaked almonds to sprinkle on top

1 Preheat the oven to 160°C/325°F/gas mark 3. Grease and line a loose-based round cake tin, 23cm (9in) in diameter, and grease the sides.

2 Place the lemon and orange zest and juice in a mixing bowl and add the oil, xylitol, eggs and almond extract. Whisk until smooth and thoroughly combined.

3 Mix the corn meal, ground almonds and baking powder together in a separate bowl. Pour the egg mixture into the dry ingredients and fold together gently until combined.

4 Pour into the prepared tin and scatter with the flaked almonds. Put the tin on a baking tray and let it stand for 10 minutes, then pop into the oven for 35–45 minutes or until pale gold at the edges and just firm to the touch in the middle.

5 Serve warm or cool on a wire rack until ready to serve.

Cook's Notes
Gluten-free, wheat-free, dairy-free, yeast-free • V • Can be made in advance – keeps in an airtight container for up to 4 days • Suitable for freezing

SPELT BISCOTTI WITH PISTACHIO AND CITRUS

Spelt is an ancient cousin to wheat, with a mild, nutty taste. It is richer in protein and fibre than wheat, as well as being much easier to digest due to its more delicate, brittle, gluten structure. This makes spelt suitable for many people who suffer from wheat intolerance or IBS. These hard biscuits are barely sweet and are just lifted by the citrus tang and the sweet dried fruit. They're perfect for dunking in peppermint tea or in an espresso after a supper party.

Makes 16

185g (6½oz) spelt flour plus a little extra for rolling

75g (3oz) xylitol

½ tsp baking powder (gluten free if necessary)

1 large free-range or organic egg, beaten

finely grated zest of 1 orange

75g (3oz) mixed dried fruit

75g (3oz) unsalted pistachios, shelled, but preferably with their skins on

2 drops of almond extract

1 Preheat the oven to 180°C/350°F/gas mark 4. Line a baking tray with baking paper.

2 Mix the flour, xylitol and baking powder together in a mixing bowl. Stir in half of the egg and mix. Then slowly mix in the remaining egg to create large breadcrumbs.

3 Stir in the orange zest, dried fruit and nuts, and bring the mixture together into a ball, using your hands, making sure that the fruit and nuts are evenly distributed. Taste and add a couple of drops of almond extract if you wish.

4 Roll the dough out on a lightly floured board and shape into a long, even sausage, around 20cm (8in) long. Flatten slightly to create the characteristic squashed shape of biscotti, then place on the baking tray and bake for around 25 minutes until golden. Remove from the oven and leave to cool for at least 15 minutes (you will need the oven again) before cutting it into 16 slices.

5 Lay the slices out on the baking tray and return to the oven for 10 minutes, then turn the slices over and cook for a further 10 minutes, to harden and turn them golden. Cool on a wire rack before storing in an airtight container for at least a week.

Cook's Notes

Wheat-free, dairy-free, yeast-free • V • Can be made in advance • Suitable for freezing

CHOCOLATE ALMOND APRICOTS

This is another healthy but delicious alternative to after-dinner mints. Very quick and easy to make, these petit fours also provide a powerful nutrient punch, as apricots are rich in the antioxidant pro-vitamin betacarotene, needed for a strong immune system and healthy skin, while almonds are rich in protein, as well as the bone-friendly minerals calcium and magnesium.

Makes 15

50g (2oz) good quality chocolate

15 ready-to-eat dried apricots

15 almonds

1 Line a baking tray or large plate with baking paper. Gently melt the chocolate over a bain marie (see page 153, step 1) or in the microwave.

2 Meanwhile, make a slit down one side of each apricot and push your finger in to create a pocket. Insert an almond inside each apricot, then dip one half of the apricot – the open half where the almond was inserted – in the melted chocolate to seal the pocket.

3 Place on the baking tray and chill in the fridge for at least half an hour until the chocolate has hardened. Store in an airtight tin in a cool, dry place.

Cook's Notes

Gluten-free, wheat-free, dairy-free • V • Can be made in advance

WHAT'S YOUR CUP OF TEA?

Unless your guests are as health-conscious as you are, you may wish to have normal black tea, milk and sugar available for afternoon tea parties, but there is no reason why you cannot offer some naturally caffeine-free, healthy herbal alternatives as well:

REDBUSH TEA (also known as Rooibos tea) is a South African leaf tea which is naturally caffeine-free and has a strong, robust flavour and colour that, unlike most herbal brews, can hold its own if you add milk or lemon, although you can also just serve it as it is. It is very rich in antioxidant flavonoids.

GREEN TEA is another strong-flavoured leaf tea, which, although caffeinated, has much less caffeine than standard black tea and is high in polyphenols, which are powerful antioxidants. It also aids the liver's detoxification process (see page 55 for more information on its health properties). To reduce the caffeine content, steep the tea in boiling water for 30 seconds, then discard the water and brew the tea afresh. You'll find that this makes the tea much less bitter as well. You can also find green tea flavoured with mint or lemon.

PEPPERMINT TEA is the traditional digestive tonic and is now increasingly available in restaurants and cafés. A pot of mint tea, ideally made with a large bunch of fresh mint from the garden, checked for bugs first, or from a tea bag, makes a very refreshing drink with sweet foods like cakes or chocolates after a dinner party.

CHAMOMILE TEA has long been used as a relaxant. It can aid sleep and is a very calming drink if you've had a stressful day.

ROSEHIP TEA is made from the hips or pods that form at the base of the rose flower. Rose hips make a very nice herbal tea and the health benefits are excellent. Rosehip tea has a pleasant, slightly tart, yet fragrant flavour and is a superb source of vitamin C as well as vitamins A, D and E and flavonoids. It is a traditional remedy for bladder infections and can be used to ease headaches.

SPICED FLAPJACKS

The mixed spice and mixed dried fruit give these sticky flapjacks a festive flavour. I use agave syrup in preference to golden syrup as it has a naturally low GL, which makes for fewer blood sugar upsets. I also add almonds, not only for flavour, but to contribute protein and minerals like calcium and magnesium as well.

Makes 10

75g (3oz) slightly salted butter

1 tbsp agave syrup

75g (3oz) mixed dried fruit

100g (4oz) whole rolled oats

50g (2oz) ground almonds

4 tsp mixed spice

1 Preheat the oven to 170°C/325°F/gas mark 3. Line a baking tray with baking paper.

2 Melt the butter and syrup together gently, taking care not to let them boil. Stir in the mixed dried fruit, oats, almonds and mixed spice.

3 Shape the mixture into ten walnut-sized balls and place on the baking tray. Bake for around 20 minutes or until just turning golden on top.

4 Leave to harden and cool on a wire rack.

Cook's Notes

Wheat-free • V • Can be made in advance • Suitable for freezing

CHOCOLATE HAZELNUT BROWNIES

Like all good brownies, these are soft and gooey. The recipe uses ground almonds instead of flour to make it gluten-free, and bananas for natural sweetness and moisture to help cut down on the amount of fat and added sugar required. It is also rich in protein from the nuts and eggs, which help slow down the release of sugar from the chocolate, as well as being good sources of B vitamins that will help put you in a good mood – as if you need extra help with brownies at hand!

Makes 12

100g (4oz) good quality dark chocolate (70 per cent cocoa solids for flavour) for melting plus 50g (2oz) finely chopped into chips

150g (5$^{1}/_{2}$oz) coconut oil, butter or dairy-free margarine suitable for baking, at room temperature

100g (4oz) xylitol

2 ripe bananas, mashed

4 large eggs, preferably free-range or organic, beaten

2 tsp vanilla extract (not artificial vanilla flavouring)

150g (5$^{1}/_{2}$oz) ground almonds

2 tsp baking powder (gluten-free if necessary)

25g (1oz) cocoa powder

200g (7oz) hazelnuts, chopped

1 Preheat the oven to 180°C/350°F/gas mark 4. Line a 22cm (9in) square baking tin with baking paper.

2 Melt the 100g of chocolate over a bain marie (see page 153, step 1) or in the microwave.

3 Cream the oil, butter or margarine and xylitol until soft and fluffy, then either blend in the rest of the ingredients in a food processor or, to do it by hand: beat in the chocolate, bananas, beaten eggs and vanilla extract then stir in the chocolate chips, ground almonds, baking powder, cocoa powder and chopped hazelnuts.

4 Pour the mixture into the prepared tin and bake for around 20 minutes or until the mixture no longer wobbles when shaken and the top is just firm to the touch. You don't want to cook it for too long or the brownies will lose their squidgy quality. Leave to cool then cut into slices for serving.

Cook's Notes
Gluten-free if you use gluten-free baking powder, wheat-free, dairy-free if you use coconut oil or dairy-free margarine, yeast-free • V • Suitable for freezing • Can be made in advance

COCONUT OAT BISCUITS

These crumbly biscuits are inspired by Australia's much loved Anzac biscuits, which combine oats with coconut. The ground ginger used here gives them a warming flavour. Agave syrup comes from the cactus plant and has a naturally low GL, to avoid upsetting blood sugar levels.

Makes 10

75g (3oz) coconut oil, butter or dairy-free margarine suitable for baking

25g (1oz) xylitol

1 tbsp agave syrup

100g (4oz) whole rolled oats

50g (2oz) desiccated coconut

1–2 tsp ground ginger (optional)

1 Preheat the oven to 170°C/325°F/gas mark 3. Line a baking tray with baking paper.

2 Gently melt the oil, butter or margarine and xylitol with the syrup, taking care not to let it boil. Stir in the oats, coconut and ginger.

3 Shape the mixture into ten walnut-sized balls. The mixture will be very crumbly at this stage, so press it together firmly then place the biscuits on the baking tray.

4 Bake for around 20 minutes or until they're just turning golden on top. Leave to harden and cool on a wire rack.

Cook's Notes

Wheat-free, dairy-free if you use coconut oil • V • Can be made in advance • Suitable for freezing

CHOCOLATE COURGETTE CAKE

This is a rich, gooey, chocolatey cake with no hint of the courgettes that lie within and it's a firm favourite in my family. The courgettes provide fibre to help offset the sugar load from the chocolate and, together with the oil, make the cake very moist.

Serves 10

200g (7oz) plain flour

1/2 tsp bicarbonate of soda

1 tsp baking powder (gluten-free if necessary)

1/2 tsp salt

100g (4oz) xylitol

2 medium free-range or organic eggs

180ml (6fl oz) mild or medium olive oil

170g (just under 6oz) good quality dark chocolate

225g (8oz) courgettes

55g (just over 2oz) walnuts, finely chopped

For the cream cheese frosting

250g (9oz) low-fat cream cheese

1/2 tsp vanilla extract

1 tbsp xylitol

1 Preheat the oven to 180°C/350°F/gas mark 4. Line a 20cm (8in) loose-bottomed cake tin with baking paper and grease the sides.

2 Sift the flour, bicarbonate of soda, baking powder and salt into a bowl. Stir in the xylitol.

3 In a separate bowl, beat the eggs into the oil.

4 Melt the chocolate over a bain marie (see page 153, step 1) or in the microwave. Meanwhile, grate the courgettes.

5 Stir the eggs and oil into the dry ingredients, then mix in the melted chocolate, courgettes and nuts.

6 Pour the mixture into the prepared cake tin and bake for 25–30 minutes or until the cake is well risen, firm to the touch and a skewer comes out clean. Allow to cool on a wire rack before icing.

7 To make the cream cheese frosting, mix together the cream cheese, vanilla extract and xylitol until smooth then spread on the cake. Store in an airtight container in the fridge.

Cook's Notes

V • Can be made in advance • Suitable for freezing, but don't ice the cake until it has defrosted

PEAR AND COCONUT CAKE

A gluten-, sugar- and dairy-free treat, this is a very unusual cake that's made entirely without flour. It gets its bulk from the desiccated coconut, while the pear makes it wonderfully moist. Coconut helps the thyroid and immune system, and although it is rich in saturated fat, it is a type of fat that is used as energy, rather than being stored as fat.

Serves 10

3 pears

250g (9oz) desiccated coconut

$1/2$ tsp baking powder (gluten-free
   if necessary)

3 medium free-range or organic eggs

150g ($5^1/2$oz) xylitol

1 Preheat the oven to 180°C/350°F/gas mark 4. Line a 20cm (8in) cake tin with baking paper and grease the sides with a little oil or butter.

2 Core the pears and pureé them in a blender.

3 Mix the desiccated coconut and baking powder in a bowl. Stir in the blended pears.

4 Beat the eggs and xylitol in a clean mixing bowl until they become pale and creamy, and start to thicken slightly – the whisk should leave a trail when lifted out of the mixture.

5 Gradually fold the pear and coconut mixture into the beaten egg, using a metal tablespoon and taking care not to knock all of the air out of the egg. It's easy to do this if you draw a figure of eight shape with the spoon as you fold.

6 Quickly pour the cake mix into the prepared tin and bake for around 50 minutes. The cake is so soft and squidgy that a skewer inserted may not come out completely clean, but when it is done the top should be golden and fairly firm to the touch. Store in an airtight container.

Cook's Notes

Gluten-free if you use gluten-free baking powder, wheat-free, dairy-free, yeast-free • V • Can be made in advance • Suitable for freezing

SPICED APPLE CAKE

Although it's similar to a Dorset apple cake, my Spiced Apple Cake is stuffed with mixed dried fruit for natural sweetness and the wonderful tang of citrus zest. Of course, the spices in this recipe add nutritional benefits as well as flavour, as ginger fights infections and inflammation, while cinnamon actually helps your body to regulate blood sugar levels. The addition of almonds provides protein to help make this cake more filling and less fattening. It's delicious for tea, but can also be served warm as a pudding with custard, vanilla ice cream or even cream.

Makes 1 loaf/10 slices

225g (8oz) self-raising wholemeal flour

3 tsp ground mixed spice

2 tsp ground cinnamon

1 large cooking apple, unpeeled, coarsely grated

150ml (5fl oz) mild or medium (not extra virgin) olive oil

75g (3oz) xylitol

1 tbsp agave syrup

1/2 tsp almond extract (not artificial almond essence)

50g (2oz) dried mixed fruit

2 large free-range or organic eggs, lightly beaten

100g (4oz) flaked almonds, roughly chopped, plus 25g (1oz) flaked almonds for sprinkling on top

1 Preheat the oven to 150°C/300°F/gas mark 2. Line a 22 x 12 x 6.5cm (2lb) loaf tin with baking paper.

2 Sift the flour, mixed spice and cinnamon into a mixing bowl (tip any leftover grains from the flour back into the mixture). Add the grated apple, oil, xylitol, syrup, almond extract, dried mixed fruit, eggs and 100g of almonds. Stir well until it's all mixed together, then scrape into the prepared tin. Scatter the remaining flaked almonds on top.

3 Bake in the centre of the oven for 1–1 1/4 hours or until the top feels fairly hard and the mixture doesn't wobble when the tin is shaken. Leave to cool on a wire rack, then store in an airtight container.

Cook's Notes

Dairy-free, yeast-free • V • Can be made in advance • Suitable for freezing

AUTUMN TEA BREAD

This tea loaf is full to bursting with warming autumnal flavours such as mixed spice and dried mixed fruit – plus the hidden addition of butternut squash, which works in the same way as grated carrot does in a carrot cake, giving a moist, naturally sweet flavour and texture, not to mention plenty of fibre and the antioxidant vitamin beta-carotene.

Makes 1 loaf/10 slices

225g (8oz) self-raising wholemeal flour
1¹/₂–2 tbsp ground mixed spice
300g (10¹/₂oz) butternut squash, peeled and coarsely grated
150ml (5fl oz) mild or medium (not extra virgin) olive oil
50g (2oz) xylitol
1 tbsp agave syrup

50g (2oz) dried mixed fruit
2 large free-range or organic eggs, lightly beaten
100g (4oz) pecans or walnuts, roughly chopped

For the icing
3 tbsp tahini
1¹/₂ tbsp agave syrup
³/₄–1 tsp ground mixed spice

1 Preheat the oven to 150°C/300°F/gas mark 2. Line a 22 x 12 x 6.5cm (2lb) loaf tin with baking paper.

2 Sift the flour and mixed spice into a mixing bowl (tip any leftover grains from the flour back into the mixture). Add the grated squash, oil, xylitol, syrup, dried mixed fruit, eggs and nuts. Stir well until it's all mixed together, then scrape into the prepared tin.

3 Bake in the centre of the oven for 1¹/₄ hours or until the top feels fairly hard and the mixture doesn't wobble when the tin is shaken. Leave to cool on a wire rack before icing.

4 Mix the icing ingredients together until smooth and creamy – add a tablespoon or so of water if necessary – and then spread on top of the loaf. Store in an airtight container.

Cook's Notes
Dairy-free, yeast-free • V • Can be made in advance • Suitable for freezing

GINGER, CARROT AND WALNUT LOAF

This mildly flavoured cake makes an excellent snack for afternoon tea as it has a mild, warming ginger flavour that's not over-poweringly sweet. It is a good, less-rich choice for serving in combination with a really gooey, sweet concoction like the Chocolate Courgette Cake (see page 167). It contains oil rather than butter, making it very moist and dairy-free, for easy digestion.

Makes 1 loaf/10 slices

225g (8oz) plain wholemeal flour

1 level tsp bicarbonate of soda

2 tsp ground ginger

1 tsp cinnamon

2 large carrots, peeled and grated

150ml (5fl oz) mild or medium (not extra virgin) olive oil

100g (4oz) xylitol

100g (4oz) stem ginger in syrup, drained and very finely chopped

2 large free-range or organic eggs, lightly beaten

100g (4oz) walnuts or pecans, roughly chopped

1 Preheat the oven to 150°C/300°F/gas mark 2. Line a 22 x 12 x 6.5cm (2lb) loaf tin with baking paper.

2 Sift the flour, bicarbonate of soda, ginger and cinnamon into a mixing bowl (tip any leftover grains from the flour back into the mixture). Add the grated carrot, oil, xylitol, stem ginger, eggs and nuts. Stir well until it's all mixed together, then scrape into the prepared tin.

3 Bake in the centre of the oven for 1–1¼ hours or until the top feels fairly hard and the mixture doesn't wobble when the tin is shaken. Leave to cool on a wire rack, then store in an airtight container.

Cook's Notes

Dairy-free, yeast-free • V • Can be made in advance • Suitable for freezing

CANAPÉS AND NIBBLES

The following ideas would all make good buffet or drinks party canapés, and are all quick and easy to prepare, as well as having plenty of eye appeal. It goes without saying that they are much healthier than the usual brigade of canapé offerings. How many you choose to serve is entirely up to you, but as a rule of thumb it's nice to offer at least six different types of canapés. Aim to provide seven canapés per person for a drink's party.

SMOKED SALMON SANDWICHES

Spread pumpernickel-style rye bread or thinly sliced wholemeal bread with cream cheese. Add thinly sliced cucumber and top with smoked salmon slices. Squeeze with lemon juice and sprinkle with black pepper, then cut into bite-sized squares.

BAKED PITTA SQUARES

Preheat the oven to 240°C/475°F/gas mark 9, then spread one side of wholemeal pitta breads with a tomato-based pasta sauce, sun-dried tomato paste or tomato purée. Top with any of the following pizza toppings: cherry tomatoes, sliced mushrooms, sliced courgette, diced peppers, pitted black olives, cooked chicken goujons, cooked prawns, strips of lean (unprocessed) ham, sliced mozzarella, grated Cheddar or Parmesan shavings.

Cook for 10 minutes or until the pitta is crispy and the vegetables have softened or the cheese melted, as appropriate. You can also add a drizzle of extra virgin olive oil, torn fresh basil leaves or dried oregano and a sprinkle of freshly ground black pepper, before cutting into bite-sized squares.

FILLED LITTLE GEM LEAVES

Break off the leaves from a Little Gem lettuce and place a spoonful of Hummus (see page 87) or Guacamole (see page 89) or Greek Salad (see page 100) inside. Sprinkle with a few freshly chopped chives or, for the Greek Salad, some dried oregano.

FETA, CUCUMBER AND OLIVE STICKS

Cut fairly thick slices of cucumber and top with a cube of feta cheese and a pitted olive or a sun-blush tomato.

GRILLED COURGETTE ROLLS WITH FETA AND SUN-BLUSH TOMATO

Prepare the Marinated Griddled Courgettes (see page 145). Place a pitted olive or a piece of sun-blush tomato and a fresh basil leaf at one end of each strip and roll up. Secure with a cocktail stick. Other filling ideas include cubes of feta with basil and/or an olive and a piece of sun-blush tomato. You should get around 12 long strips from each courgette, so two courgettes would serve four people, providing six pieces each.

TOASTED SEEDS

Lightly toast pumpkin and/or sunflower seeds in a large, dry frying pan for 2–3 minutes until they just start to turn crisp and pop. Season with a little tamari, soy sauce or sea salt. A tasty alternative to crisps without the high fat and starch content, these are also rich in protein and minerals such as zinc, to help skin condition and libido!

SPICED CASHEW NUTS

Preheat the oven to 170°C/325°F/gas mark 3. Scatter 200g (7oz) of raw, unsalted cashew nuts on a baking tray and drizzle with a tablespoon of mild or medium (not extra extra virgin) olive oil. Sprinkle with a teaspoon each of mild curry powder, smoked paprika and a pinch of salt, then roast for 15 minutes, shaking the tray to turn them over halfway through. Leave to cool then taste, adding a little more salt if necessary. These are a spicy alternative to the ubiquitous peanuts and crisps.

MARINATED CHICKEN SKEWERS

Marinate bite-sized pieces of chicken in tamari or soy sauce, grated fresh ginger and lime or lemon juice for an hour if possible. Then thread the chicken onto metal or bamboo skewers (if using bamboo, pre-soak in water for 30 minutes to prevent the wood from burning) along with cubes of vegetables, such as pepper, mushroom, red onion or spring onion. Brush the kebabs with the residual marinade to coat the vegetables, before cooking under a hot grill for around 10 minutes or until the meat is cooked through (the juices should run clear) and the vegetables have softened.

DRINKS

The following recipes are all soft drinks, but to cater for everyone you can add alcohol to most of them. These are some much healthier, more natural alternatives to the sugary, artificial flavours of many alcopops or soft drinks on the market. They all include fruit, which will provide vitamins to help your liver cope with any alcohol, as well as cutting out the need for sugary mixers. Far be it from me to dictate how much you drink, but as with all things, moderation is the key. If you're drinking alcohol, try to match each glass with a soft drink or a glass of water, to slow down your rate of consumption and keep your body hydrated, as this will lessen any hangover in the morning.

LEMONADE

Using the safe sugar substitute xylitol makes this refreshing drink sugar-free, plus the fresh lemon juice provides plenty of vitamin C. You can add a shot of vodka if you like.

Serves 4

juice of 2 lemons

2 tbsp xylitol

800ml (29fl oz) naturally sparkling mineral water

1 Stir all the ingredients together until the xylitol dissolves.

2 Pour into tall glasses, and serve with ice and a slice of lemon.

Cook's Notes

Gluten-free, wheat-free, dairy-free, yeast-free • V • Can be made in advance, but don't add the sparkling water until ready to serve

RASPBERRY REFRESHER

Raspberries are very rich in flavonoids, the plant-based antioxidants that help fight infection and stave off age-related diseases.

Serves 4

400g (14oz) raspberries

4 bananas

400ml (just over 13fl oz) water

xylitol to taste, if the berries are very tart

1 Blend all the ingredients until smooth, then taste and sweeten if necessary.

2 Serve fresh or chilled with ice.

Cook's Notes

Gluten-free, wheat-free, dairy-free, yeast-free • V • Can be made in advance and chilled until required

WATERMELON WHIZ

With its high water content, watermelon is perhaps the most refreshing of summer fruits. It is also very rich in betacarotene to keep eyes and skin healthy. Keep the seeds in as they blend into the smoothie and are packed with vitamin E.

Serves 4

4 large slices of watermelon, rind removed

1 Blend the watermelon flesh, seeds and all, until smooth.

2 Pour into glasses and serve with ice or blend the ice with the watermelon for an instant chilled juice.

Cook's Notes

Gluten-free, wheat-free, dairy-free, yeast-free • V

BLOODY/VIRGIN MARY

This classic cocktail can be enjoyed equally by drinkers and drivers alike if you serve two versions, but be careful not to confuse them! The tomato juice provides plenty of the antioxidant lycopene, which helps protect your skin from UV damage from the sun – ideal in warm weather.

Serves 4

4 shots of vodka (omit for a Virgin Mary)

600ml (1pt) tomato juice

juice of half a lemon

a good slug of Tabasco or hot pepper sauce

a good slug of Worcestershire sauce

celery salt or sea salt, to taste, depending on tomato juice seasoning

freshly ground black pepper

2 sticks of celery, cut in half

1 Place ice in four short glasses and add a shot of vodka, if using, to each one.

2 Pour in the tomato juice, lemon juice, Tabasco and Worcestershire sauce and stir. Add salt and pepper, and adjust the seasoning to taste, then add a stick of celery to each glass before serving.

Cook's Notes

Gluten-free, wheat-free, dairy-free, yeast-free • V • Can be made in advance

CARIBBEAN COCKTAIL

The fat from coconuts is used as energy rather than being stored as fat, making this a much better choice than cream-based cocktails, but shake the coconut milk can before opening as it separates. Bananas are also excellent for digestion. Add rum for a more authentic Caribbean drink.

Serves 4

4 bananas

600ml (1pt) coconut milk

12 ice cubes

1 Blend all the ingredients together, pour into short glasses and drink immediately.

Cook's Notes

Gluten-free, wheat-free, dairy-free, yeast-free • V

BELLINI

This is a refreshing, sweet taste of summer, which can be adapted to make it non-alcoholic for drivers or those trying to be good. The peaches add vitamin C, B vitamins and betacarotene, which help to protect the liver and go some way to compensating for the alcohol load!

Serves 4

2 large ripe peaches

2 heaped tbsp raspberries

1 bottle chilled Champagne or non-alcoholic, sparkling grape juice

1 Chill the glasses.

2 Pureé the peaches until completely smooth. If necessary, you can do this in advance and chill the pureé. Press the raspberries through a fine sieve to extract the pulp without the seeds. Again, you can do this in advance and put the pulp in the fridge.

3 Place a couple of tablespoons of the peach purée and a teaspoon of raspberry purée into each glass and slowly top up with wine or juice, stirring as you pour. You should aim to have one-third fruit purée to two-thirds fizz.

Cook's Notes

Gluten-free, wheat-free, dairy-free, yeast-free • V

STRAWBERRIES AND CREAM

I can honestly say this is summer in a glass. This sweet, fruity drink is rich in fibre, vitamin C and flavonoids from the berries, and the milk makes it much lower in fat than a cream-based cocktail.

Serves 4

400g (14oz) strawberries, hulled

400ml (just over 13fl oz) semi-skimmed milk or non-dairy milk

2–4 tbsp xylitol to taste

1 Blend the strawberries and milk together until smooth. Taste and add xylitol if it's not sweet enough.

2 Pour into short glasses and serve.

Cook's Notes

Gluten-free, wheat-free, dairy-free if you use non-dairy milk, yeast-free • V • Can be made in advance and chilled until required

Resources

General

Nutrition Consultancy in Commercial Catering

The Russell Partnership, the UK's leading strategic catering and hospitality consultancy, offers advice and assistance on the Commercial Application of Nutrition. Services include Nutritional Audits, leading to Food for the Brain accreditation, training and workshops on the Commercial Application of Nutrition. Visit www.russellpartnership.com or call +44 (0) 20 7665 1888 for more details.

Institute for Optimum Nutrition (ION)

ION runs courses including a home-study course and a three-year, part-time Nutrition Therapy foundation degree. For details on courses, consultations and publications visit www.ion.ac.uk or call +44 (0)20 8614 7800.

Nutrition consultations

The British Association for Applied Nutrition & Therapy (BANT) has a list of nutritional therapists. Tel: 0870 606 1284 or visit www.bant.org.uk. In Ireland, see the Nutritional Therapist of Ireland at www.ntoi.ie. In South Africa, see the South African Association of Nutritional Therapists www.saant.org.za.

Nutrition assessment online

You can have your own personal health and nutrition assessment online using Patrick Holford's 100% Health Check. This gives you a personalised assessment of your current health, and what you most need to change. Visit www.patrickholford.com and go to 'free health check'.

Psychocalisthenics

Psychocalisthenics is an excellent exercise system that takes less than 20 minutes a day, develops strength, suppleness and stamina, and generates vital energy. For further information, see www.pcals.com. For training in the UK, visit www.integralview.org. You can also teach yourself using the Psychocalisthenics DVD, available from www.pcals.com or www.patrickholford.com.

Foods

Low-GL Foods

Specialist low-GL foods, including chocolate and pasta, are available from www.patrickholford.com.

Cacao (raw chocolate powder) and other 'superfoods'

Detox Your World imports raw, organic superfoods such as cacao (raw chocolate powder) for wholesale across Europe. You can find the Detox Your World range in good whole food shops and online at www.detoxyourworld.com.

Sugar alternatives – xylitol

While it is best to avoid sugar and sugar alternatives as much as possible, xylitol has a GL score one-ninth that of regular sugar and tastes the same. It is available across the UK in health shops and some supermarkets under the brand name Total Sweet. Visit www.totalsweet.co.uk for stockists.

Salt alternatives – Solo low sodium sea salt

The average person gets far too much sodium because we eat too much salt (sodium chloride) and salted foods, and not enough potassium and magnesium, found in fruits and vegetables. Not all salt, however, is bad for you. Solo low sodium sea salt contains 60 per cent less sodium and is high in the essential minerals magnesium and potassium. Solo low sodium sea salt is sold in UK, Ireland, Spain, the Netherlands, Singapore, Hong Kong, Japan, Bahrain, Saudi Arabia, United Arab Emirates, Jordan, Baltic States and United States of America. Visit their website: www.soloseasalt.com for more information.

Tests

Food intolerance

YorkTest Laboratories sells FoodScan, a mail-order, food-intolerance test. It is a finger-prick test, with the added benefit of a clinical laboratory analysis. Designed as a simple two-step process, the First Step FoodScan is an indicator test that will generate a positive or negative result. If positive, your sample is then upgraded to the Second Step FoodScan 113 Test, a comprehensive service that tests for 113 foods. This identifies the foods causing the intolerance and the level of intolerance. In addition, the service includes nutritionist consultations and comprehensive support and advice on managing your elimination diet. Call YorkTest Laboratories on 0800 130 0580 or visit www.yorktest.com.

Recommended Reading

Patrick Holford, *The Optimum Nutrition Bible*, Piatkus (2004).

Patrick Holford and Judy Ridgway, *The Optimum Nutrition Cookbook*, Piatkus (2001).

Patrick Holford and Fiona McDonald Joyce, *The Holford Low-GL Diet Cookbook*, Piatkus (2006).

Patrick Holford and Fiona McDonald Joyce, *Smart Food for Smart Kids*, Piatkus (2007).

Patrick Holford and Fiona McDonald Joyce, *The Holford 9-day Liver Detox*, Piatkus (2007).

References

1. D. Jenkins, American Journal of Clinical Nutrition, (2006).

2. Hourigan, C.S., 'The molecular basis of celiac disease', *Clinical and Experimental Medicine*, Vol. 6(2) 2006, pp. 53–9.

3. Sandiford, C.P., et al., 'Identification of the major water/salt insoluble wheat proteins involved in cereal hypersensitivity', *Clinical and Experimental Allergy*, Vol. 27 (1997), pp. 1120–9.

4. Stoersrud, S., et al., 'Adult coeliac disease patients do tolerate large amounts of oats', *European Journal of Clinical Nutrition*, Vol. 57 (2003), pp. 163–9 and Hoegberg, L., et al., 'Oats to children with newly diagnosed coeliac disease: a randomised double blind study', *Gut*, Vol. 54 (2004), pp. 645–54.

5. osiris.sunderland.ac.uk/autism/

6. www.greatplainslaboratory.com/russian/glutencasein.html and osiris.sunderland.ac.uk/autism/aru.htm

7. US National Institutes of Health, digestive.niddk.nih.gov/ddiseases/pubs/lactoseintolerance/

8. LeRoith, D., Roberts Jr., C.T., 'The insulin-like growth factor system and cancer', *Cancer Letters*, Vol. 195(2) (10 June 2003), pp. 127–37. Review.

Index

patrick HOLFORD
100% HEALTH WORKSHOPS

TOTAL HEALTH TRANSFORMATION

Avoid the mid-life health meltdown. Beat the bulge. Give your body a total transformation. Find out how to radically improve your health in this highly informative and motivating workshop. You leave with your own personalised health plan and the tools to be successful.

OPTIMUM EXERCISE IN 15 MINUTES

How do you keep fit, strong, supple and full of energy? The habit of exercise can be hard to keep up, but how much easier would it be if all you needed was 15 minutes every day? This workshop shows you four simple ways to achieve these goals in 15 minutes a day.

OPTIMUM NUTRITION FOR THE MIND

There is no need to have declining energy, memory, motivation and mood. In this one-day workshop you will learn everything Patrick's learnt in 35 years exploring nutrition for mental health.

THE POWER OF CONNECTION

Is life an adventure or an ordeal? Are you having a good time, full of 'joie de vivre' or are you bored or in discomfort of one sort or another, be it emotional or mental anguish, stress or physical pain? Does life make sense or do you have the feeling there's another level of existence but don't know how to get there? Patrick Holford shares deepest wisdoms that help you feel fully alive and awake and connected on all levels, living a purposeful life.

For latest seminars and workshops visit
www.patrickholford.com/events